DATE DUE

CONTEMPORARY WRITERS

General Editors
MALCOLM BRADBURY
and
CHRISTOPHER BIGSBY

GÜNTER GRASS

IN THE SAME SERIES

Donald Barthelme   *M. Couturier and R. Durand*
Saul Bellow   *Malcolm Bradbury*
Richard Brautigan   *Marc Chénetier*
E. L. Doctorow   *Paul Levine*
Margaret Drabble   *Joanne V. Creighton*
John Fowles   *Peter Conradi*
Graham Greene   *John Spurling*
Seamus Heaney   *Blake Morrison*
Ted Hughes   *Thomas West*
Philip Larkin   *Andrew Motion*
Doris Lessing   *Lorna Sage*
Malcolm Lowry   *Ronald Binns*
David Mamet   *C. W. E. Bigsby*
Iris Murdoch   *Richard Todd*
Joe Orton   *C. W. E. Bigsby*
Harold Pinter   *G. Almansi and S. Henderson*
Thomas Pynchon   *Tony Tanner*
Alain Robbe-Grillet   *John Fletcher*
Philip Roth   *Hermione Lee*
Kurt Vonnegut   *Jerome Klinkowitz*
Patrick White   *John Colmer*

For Anna

First published in 1985 by
Methuen & Co. Ltd
11 New Fetter Lane, London EC4P 4EE
Published in the USA by
Methuen & Co.
in association with Methuen, Inc.
29 West 35th Street, New York, NY 10001

Typeset by Rowland Phototypesetting Ltd
Printed in Great Britain by
Richard Clay (The Chaucer Press) Ltd
Bungay, Suffolk

British Library Cataloguing in Publication Data

Hayman, Ronald
Günter Grass. – (Contemporary writers)
1. Grass, Günter – Criticism and interpretation
I. Title. II. Series
833'.914   PT2613.R338Z/

ISBN 0-416-35490-4

Library of Congress Cataloging in Publication Data

Hayman, Ronald, 1932–
Günter Grass.
(Contemporary writers)
Bibliography: p.
1. Grass, Günter, 1927–   – Criticism and interpretation.
I. Title.   II. Series.
PT2613.R338Z664   1985   838'.91409   85-11446

ISBN 0-416-35490-4 (pbk.)

GÜNTER
GRASS

RONALD HAYMAN

METHUEN
LONDON AND NEW YORK

CONTENTS

General editors' preface   6
Acknowledgements   8
A note on the texts and translations   9

Introduction: Disinfectant literature   10
1   Puppets and ballerinas   13
2   Windfowls and talking rats   23
3   Drums and eels   29
4   Cats and dogs   44
5   Teeth and snails   56
6   Floundering   65
7   Creativity and procreation   69

Notes   76
Bibliography   77

GENERAL EDITORS' PREFACE

The contemporary is a country which we all inhabit, but there is little agreement as to its boundaries or its shape. The serious writer is one of its most sensitive interpreters, but criticism is notoriously cautious in offering a response or making a judgement. Accordingly, this continuing series is an endeavour to look at some of the most important writers of our time, and the questions raised by their work. It is, in effect, an attempt to map the contemporary, to describe its aesthetic and moral topography.

The series came into existence out of two convictions. One was that, despite all the modern pressures on the writer and on literary culture, we live in a major creative time, as vigorous and alive in its distinctive way as any that went before. The other was that, though criticism itself tends to grow more theoretical and apparently indifferent to contemporary creation, there are grounds for a lively aesthetic debate. This series, which includes books written from various standpoints, is meant to provide a forum for that debate. By design, some of those who have contributed are themselves writers, willing to respond to their contemporaries; others are critics who have brought to the discussion of current writing the spirit of contemporary criticism or simply a conviction, forcibly and coherently argued, for the contemporary significance of their subjects. Our aim, as the series develops, is to continue to explore the works of major post-war writers – in fiction, drama and poetry – over an international range, and thereby to illuminate not only those works but also in some degree the artistic, social and moral assumptions on which they rest. Our wish is that, in their very variety of approach and emphasis, these books will stimulate interest in and understanding of the vitality of a living literature which, because it is contemporary, is especially ours.

Norwich, England   MALCOLM BRADBURY
                                                 CHRISTOPHER BIGSBY

ACKNOWLEDGEMENTS

This book would not be what it is but for Judith Bumpus, who coincidentally commissioned me, just before I started it, to script and present a 45-minute radio feature on Grass. I am greatly indebted to her and to those who contributed interviews to the programme in London, Paris, Hamburg, Tübingen, Munich and (by means of simultaneous recording) Norfolk and New York – Walter Abish, Reinhard Baumgart, Renate Becker, Malcolm Bradbury, Eva Figes, Wolfgang Hildesheimer, Ralph Manheim, Hans Mayer, Fritz Raddatz and Volker Schlöndorff. Professor Mayer gave me copies of his book *Aussenseiter* and of Franz Josef Görtz's book *Günter Grass: Auskunft für Leser*. When I was in Vancouver, Patrick O'Neill gave me a copy of his *Günter Grass: A Bibliography 1955–75* and an offprint of his essay 'The Scheherezade Syndrome: Günter Grass's Meganovel *Der Butt*'.

For all this kindness and co-operation I am most grateful.

The author and publishers would like to thank Secker & Warburg Ltd and Random House, Inc. for permission to reproduce copyright material from *The Tin Drum*.

A NOTE ON THE TEXTS AND TRANSLATIONS

Page references for quotations from Günter Grass's works are to the hardback editions of *Cat and Mouse, Dog Years, Local Anaesthetic* and *The Flounder*, and to the Penguin editions of *The Tin Drum, From the Diary of a Snail, The Meeting at Telgte, Headbirths* and *Four Plays*.

All these were translated by Ralph Manheim. Translations from Grass's verse and from his untranslated essays are my own. The following abbreviations have been used:

TD *The Tin Drum*
CM *Cat and Mouse*
DY *Dog Years*
LA *Local Anaesthetic*
DS *From the Diary of a Snail*
F *The Flounder*
MT *The Meeting at Telgte*
H *Headbirths*
FP *Four Plays*
GG *Gesammelte Gedichte*

INTRODUCTION: DISINFECTANT
LITERATURE

In September 1939, when the war began, Günter Grass was not quite 12. Brought up in Danzig as a member of the lower middle class, which responded gullibly and greedily to the promises implicit in Nazi ideology, he had joined the *Jungvolk* at the age of 10, and progressed into the Hitler Youth. When he was 15 he still wanted – and was still allowed – to sit on his mother's lap,[1] but he was not yet 17 when he became a soldier. He fought as a gunner in a tank regiment on the Eastern front and then in the battle for Berlin until he was wounded in 1945 and captured by the Americans. He was not troubled by any doubts about whether he was doing the right thing until, together with other young Germans from the prison camp, he was taken to see the concentration camp at Dachau. At first he was incredulous: had the evidence been faked by the Americans to discredit their defeated enemy? But when the Nüremberg Trials began, he heard German radio reporters talking about Nazi war crimes.[2] It was no longer possible to believe in the values or in the version of reality he had learned from the grown-ups. If the 15-year-old Günter Grass had still been a child, he came of age when he was pitched vertiginously into thinking for himself. It seemed as if the whole generation of adults had been a generation of betrayers – as trustworthy as werewolves. The history of civilization in Germany had led to the concentration camps.

In 1946, when he was released from prison camp at the age of 19, he was a long way from being ready to start *The Tin Drum* (which was to appear in 1959) while the Germans were a long way from being ready to read it. The country, ravaged by desperate fighting and ruthless air raids, was sectioned up by the victorious Allies; the people were exhausted, bereaved, impoverished, disoriented, fearful about the future. National hubris and optimism had been reversed into humiliation. In private, stories could be told about personal experience, but the strenuous cult of 'Denazification' was more conducive to fictions that were given factual status than to fiction as an art. Even if literary traditions had not been disrupted, long before the war began, by the book-burning Nazis, with their rabid anti-Semitism and their misconceptions about what constituted degeneracy, it would have been hard for the novel to thrive in a soil soured by shame and self-pity.

Expressionism was a force that the Nazis had failed to extirpate and it flickered back into Wolfgang Borchert's 1947 play *The Man Outside*. After being wounded on the Russian front, and being condemned to death – for defeatism – by the Nazis, Borchert was entitled to repudiate his evil leaders, but it is doubtful whether he would ever have achieved a literary equilibrium, even if he had not died, prematurely, later in 1947. Though it had looked like a sign of health, the brightness in the prose was feverish.

Of the writers who had fought in the German army, Heinrich Böll, who published his first novel in 1949, was most successful in channelling his experiences into fiction. The war served him first as a subject and later as a model for all the destructive, unanalysable forces which uncontrollably subvert our attempts to create democratic social structures, conducive to tolerance and progress. His early novels are the best examples of *Trümmerliteratur* – the literature that describes the ruins left by the fighting. The temptation, for the German novelist, was to make the dissident and the deserter into romantic heroes, but Böll avoided this mistake, though the lamb-like deserter, Feinhals, in his 1951 novel *And Where*

Were You Adam? is the first in a long line of sympathetic deserters who appear in his fiction.

As a Catholic, Böll had a set of clearly defined values, but the German language had been debilitated and almost discredited by the ideology it had appeared to nurture. Nazism, as he said, 'has infected our thinking, contaminated the air we breathe, the words we speak and write'. His commitment was founded on his belief that conscience and language had been separated: it was now for the writer to make sure that this never happened again, and the proper vigilance was incompatible with the amnesia that was so endemic: 'We live in a land that has repressed its history, the war, the persecution of the Jews.' Unfortunately a sense of responsibility is no defence against the rhetoric that righteousness can inspire.

Böll did well to break free from the old tradition of telling naturalistic stories about personal emotion and sexual triangles. Temperamentally he was disinclined to make formal experiments, but several pressures combined to heighten his awareness that narrative should look critically at the narrative act. During the period of 'Denazification' many of those who had been active in the Party evaded punishment by producing written reports which told the truth but not the whole truth. The procedures of reporting are satirized in Böll's novel *Group Portrait with Lady*: its basic questions are about its information content and where the information comes from. Böll writes with a comically pernickety insistence on citing sources for each 'fact' cited in the fiction.

Ten years younger than Böll, Grass has turned out to be less committed to the novel as a form, but more important as an innovative novelist.

1

PUPPETS AND BALLERINAS

At the end of his essay 'The Ballerina', published in 1956, three years before *The Tin Drum*, Grass suggests a marriage between the puppet and the ballerina – a notion which derives from Heinrich von Kleist's 1810 essay on puppet theatre. Three months before writing it, Kleist formulated the idea in a letter: 'Every primary, involuntary movement is beautiful, while everything that understands itself is twisted, distorted. Oh reason! Miserable reason!'[3] Kleist's essay centres on a successful male dancer who recognizes that he can learn from watching puppets. While the human dancer is dragged downwards by self-consciousness and the force of gravity, the puppet – artificial but apparently airborne – can soar effortlessly, gracefully, innocently. We are all disfigured by finite knowledge; perfect elegance of movement is compatible only with unawareness or infinite awareness. We should expect it only in the puppet or the god.[4]

In Grass's variation on Kleist's theme the ballerina is dancing, muse-like, on the desk of a writer who speculates about her art. The tenor can hold on to the back of a chair to support himself; the ballerina's body is her only prop. Equilibrium is what seemingly releases her from being earthbound. 'We shall see with the pirouette, this screwed up, artificial abstraction, the ultimate gyration seems to have succeeded, that the trick is performed. Art which goes beyond nature, for here the paper

13

rose – we know them from miniature rifle-ranges – is ahead of all vegetation and never withers. And art because it is violent rebellion against the stupid, limited limbs and punctilious exercise at an empty form, once again attains to a weightless beauty without surname or Christian name.'[5] It does not matter who the dancer is. Impressed by her grace and her serene smile, the audience does not know whether her feet are hurting or whether she is worrying about a late period: she appears to have liberated herself from the force of gravity and from personal preoccupations.

The excitement Grass conveys to his readers often arises from the excitement he experiences when combining the programmatic with the cryptic while writing about artistic activity. The ballerina is exemplary: the writer too can rise out of mediocrity if he preserves an equilibrium. Grass sometimes does this by writing dialectically, and in a 1957 essay, 'Content as Resistance', he exposes the inadequacy of Wassily Kandinsky's precept: 'The properly evolved form expresses its thanks by taking care of the content without any help.'[6] Looking equally askance at the politically engaged poets of the 1950s, who set no value on form, and at the avantgardistes who set no value on meaning, Grass proposed 'to sew mistrust between form and content'. The central section of the essay is called 'A Mistrustful Dialogue'. The speakers are two poets. Wandering through a meadow with Krudewil, Pempelfort, an old-fashioned romantic, collects metaphors as he picks flowers, while Krudewil, irritably slashing with his stick at mole-hills, grumbles about his companion's escapism. Pempelfort's relationship with his muse is shown to depend on his habit of eating indigestible food in the late evening to induce nightmares that will yield raw material for his poetry. Krudewil, who despises dreams and fantasies, has brought knitting needles and two large balls of grey wool: 'We must knit ourselves a new muse. Grey, mistrustful, ignorant of botany, heaven and death, hard-working, erotically inarticulate and not in the least a dreamer. . . . Our new muse is an accurate housekeeper.' Looking mischievously back at the antinomy between the aestheticism

14

of Gottried Benn and the materialism of Bertolt Brecht, Grass constructs a comic dialectic of categorical imperatives, sympathizing more with Krudewil than with Pempelfort, but identifying with neither. The colour grey serves as a symbol of compromise and moderation: it represents an alternative to the black and white solutions of idealists and extremists.

Pempelfort and Krudewil had already made an appearance in Grass's second play, *Only Ten Minutes to Buffalo*, which was written in 1954. Here the paradox centres not on the vertical movement of the dancer or the puppet but on lateral movement. A rusty old railway engine had been abandoned in a field but the bullying Hardy-like Krudewil carries on as if he is the driver of a moving train, while the timorous Laurel-like Pempelfort acts as his fireman. When the train stops, he collects cow-dung to use as fuel. A painter, Kotschenreuther, has set up his easel in the field and, watched by a yokel, Axel, he is working at a picture, apparently using the engine as his model, though the painting is beginning to look like a frigate. He tells Axel:

> You've got to attune yourself to the new spirit. You've got to dive down under the old values. . . . Then you'll discover new aspects, sensitive instruments, prophetic mechanisms, a virgin continent . . . and first of all you've got to throw all these stupid titles overboard. Cow, ship, painter, buttercup. They're all delusions, hallucinations, complexes. Do you think your cow minds if you call it a sailboat . . . or even a steamer?

AXEL. You may be right. But what about my eyes? When I look and see – here a cow and there a ship . . .

KOTSCHENREUTHER. That's just it, that's the big mistake. You look at things with your intellect. Keep your simplicity, start all over again from scratch. In the beginning was the ship. Later it developed into a cow, and the cow into a chess set, then the pyramids were built, then came journalism and with it the railroad – who knows what will happen tomorrow? – Bring me some sail juice, I'm thirsty.

15

AXEL. You mean milk, sir?

KOTSCHENREUTHER. Call it whatever you like, as long as it's
as white as Moby Dick. (*FP*, pp. 129–30)

Kleist had prefigured the Surrealists' rejection of reason, and
Grass is here writing a comic manifesto for the method he had
been using in his poems, disregarding categories and leaping
exuberantly from one object or area of experience to another.

Comedy has always been more generous than tragedy in
accommodating the inconsequential, and in Grass's *nouvelle
vague* surrealism he preserves a dancer-like equilibrium between high seriousness and clowning, contriving suspense
while rejecting conventional narrative, visibly benefiting from
the advice he had offered himself in his cryptically programmatic first play, *Rocking Back and Forth: A Prelude in the
Theatre* (1954). The subtitle points to the prologue which
Goethe wrote for *Faust* and which was originally staged with
puppets. In Grass's play a clown anticipates Oskar Matzerath's
refusal to grow up or to surrender his tin drum: the clown,
Conelli, refuses to dismount from his rocking horse, despite the
eminently reasonable arguments advanced by the dramaturge,
the playwright and the actor, who try to reclaim him for the
world of adult responsibility, arguing the merits of tragedy,
comedy and the Beckettian mixture of the two – tinged with
surrealism. Besides, after Cocteau's film *Orphée*, wouldn't a
motor cycle be preferable to the rocking-horse? The playwright
introduces a bed with a woman in it, but Conelli rejects the
possibility of erotic suspense. When the playwright suggests a
violent scene, 'Rape of the Clown', Conelli feigns death, coming back to life only when his daughter introduces real-life
drama in the form of a quarrel with her boyfriend. Wanting to
develop the clown into a tragic figure, the playwright proposes to make him responsible, by neglect, for the end of the
world. He will be lynched, and the fourth act will centre on
his funeral. The clown rocks wildly to and fro, but he is
more concerned with the children's performance, which is to
follow, than with not being late for his funeral.

In *The Tin Drum* there is a great deal of obliquely programmatic artistic activity. The story has hardly begun when the narrator, an inmate in a mental hospital, raises the question of whether the male nurse, Bruno, is an artist. 'He picks up pieces of string in the patients' rooms after visiting hours, disentangles them, and works them up into elaborate contorted spooks; then he dips them in plaster, lets them harden, and mounts them on knitting needles that he fastens to little wooden pedestals' (*TD*, p. 11). Behind this is the suggestion Grass had attributed to Krudewil – that we must knit ourselves a new muse.

The Tin Drum centres on a boy who at the age of 3 decided not to grow up into what the adults had made of the environment. While his mind, already unrealistically precocious, goes on maturing, Oskar clings to his infant size and to childish pursuits. He uses his toy drum in the way other children use transitional objects, beating it whenever he needs comfort, instead of cuddling a favourite toy or clinging to a segment of quilted blanket.

As a drummer Oskar Matzerath is himself something of an artist. In 1947, apprenticed to a Düsseldorf stonemason, Grass had played the drums in a jazz band. When he went on in 1948 to study at the academy of art there, he had unequivocally committed himself to the artist's life, but uncertainty about his right to call himself an artist is revived in his characters. Is Matzerath, Oskar's putative father, an artist when he cooks? What about Meyn, the trumpeter who performs so much better when he is drunk, and Bebra, the dwarf who works in a circus as an acrobatic clown? What about Oskar's trick of shattering glass with his scream? Is this art?

In featuring the artistic process so often within the work of art, Grass, like so many post-modernist writers, is incorporating a series of mirrors in which he can glance critically for reflections of his own activity.

But we are over half-way through the novel before an artistic programme is advanced, and this time more ironically than in the early essays and plays. 'Barbaric, mystical, bored', is the title proposed by the former painter, Corporal Lankes, for his seashell and concrete decorations above the entrances to the pillboxes built among the Normandy sand dunes. Lankes assumes that the pillboxes, which were made to last, will survive the next five world wars, and that eventually an archaeologist will find these decorated pillboxes. 'He sees my Structural Oblique Formations, and he says to himself, Say, take a look at that, Very, very interesting, magic, menacing, and yet shot through with spirituality. In these works a genius, perhaps the only genius of the twentieth century, has expressed himself clearly, resolutely, and for all time.' (*TD*, p. 330). As in Krudewil's grey wool, there is presumably no colour – or almost none – in the seashells and the dull, drab concrete.

The aesthetic programme Oskar proposes for Bruno is based on the notion of combining Goethe with Rasputin. Central to Grass's work is the idea, first propounded in 'The Ballerina', that equilibrium can release us from being earthbound; the equilibrium is achieved by choosing the right point between powerful opposing forces such as Beethoven and Hitler, whose pictures hang on opposite walls of the Danzig living-room in *The Tin Drum*, or the Holy Ghost and Hitler, the objects of worship in Grass's boyhood, as he complains in the auto-biographical poem 'Kleckerburg', or Goethe and Rasputin:

I snap my fingers at Schiller and company and fluctuate between Rasputin and Goethe, between the faith healer and the man of the Enlightenment, between the dark spirit who cast a spell on women and the luminous poet prince who was so fond of letting women cast a spell on him. If for a time I inclined more towards Rasputin and feared Goethe's intoler-ance, it was because of a faint suspicion that if you, Oskar, had lived and drummed at his time, Goethe would have thought you unnatural, would have condemned you as an incarnation of anti-nature, that while feeding his own precious nature – which essentially you have always admired and striven for even when it gave itself the most unnatural airs – on honeybuns, he would have taken notice

18

of you, poor devil, only to hit you over the head with *Faust* or a big heavy volume of his *Theory of Colours*. . . . I didn't want to stake everything on Rasputin, for only too soon it became clear to me that in this world of ours every Rasputin has his Goethe, that every Rasputin draws a Goethe or if you prefer every Goethe a Rasputin in his wake, or even makes one if need be, in order to be able to condemn him later on. (*TD*, pp. 86–9)

After Bruno has constructed a number of string figures based on characters who feature in the narrative, Oskar asks him to combine Goethe and Rasputin

into a single figure which, moreover, should present a striking resemblance to himself. He even knows how many miles of string I have tied into knots, trying to create a valid synthesis of the two extremes. But like the partisan whom Mr Matzerath so admires, I remain restless and dissatisfied; what I knot with my right hand, I undo with my left, what my left hand creates, my right fist shatters. (*TD*, p. 417)

We get more detailed proposals for an aesthetic programme when Oskar after deciding to grow again, and becoming a hunchback, works briefly as a model in an art school. The students are sketching in charcoal; the teacher, Professor Kuchen, has a black beard, coal-black eyes, soft black hat and black fingernails.

What he wanted was expression, always expression, pitch-black, desperate expression. I, Oskar, he maintained, was the shattered image of man, an accusation, a challenge, timeless yet expressing the madness of our century. In conclusion he thundered over the easels: 'I don't want you to sketch this cripple, this freak of nature, I want you to slaughter him, crucify him, to nail him to your paper with charcoal!' (*TD*, p. 455)

Oskar's chestnut-brown hair and his blue eyes are reduced to colourlessness. The professor and his students draw cadaverous features which exude disapproval, condemnation; they recognize the Rasputin in Oskar, but not the dormant Goethe.

Oskar next sits for a sculptor, Maruhn, who is a lover of classical form and finds it impossible to arrange Oskar's arms satisfactorily (*TD*, pp. 457–8). In a painting class the students fail to get the colours right. Oskar's brown hair and pink mouth are rendered in macabre blues with touches of moribund green and nauseous yellow (*TD*, pp. 459–60). No satisfactory works of art are produced until Oskar is teamed with a girl, Ulla, who models for Lankes, the former corporal. Two painters, nicknamed 'Ziege' and 'Raskolnikov' get to work on them:

> colour or delicate grey tones laid on with a fine brush (Raskolnikov) or with the impetuous palette knife of genius (Ziege). Some of these paintings carried an intimation of the mystery surrounding Ulla and Oskar; they were the work of Raskolnikov, who, with our help, found his way to surrealism: Oskar's face became a honey-yellow dial like that of our grandfather clock; in my hump bloomed mechanical roses which Ulla picked; Ulla, smiling on one end and long-legged on the other, was cut open in the middle and inside sat Oskar between her spleen and liver, turning over the pages of a picture book. Sometimes they put us in costume, turning Ulla into a Columbine and me into a mournful mime covered with white grease paint. It was Raskolnikov – so nicknamed because he never stopped talking of crime and punishment, guilt and atonement – who turned out the masterpiece: I sitting on Ulla's milk-white, naked thigh, a crippled child – she was the Madonna, while I sat still for Jesus.

In post-war German literature no masterpiece could have been produced by an artist who was not preoccupied with guilt and atonement. Unlike Kuchen, Raskolnikov gives free rein to his imagination. A hunchback can become a crippled Jesus.

There are many reasons for the appeal of the ballerina to Grass's imagination. One is that his own art is essentially a balancing act. He works dialectically. Between Beethoven and Hitler, between Goethe and Rasputin, he uses the rival magnetic forces to jerk him aloft, preserving a precarious balance which might have been even more precarious if he had remained earthbound.

*

Describing the wit of the Metaphysical poets, Samuel Johnson wrote: 'The most heterogeneous ideas are yoked by violence together';[7] many of Grass's best effects depend – with a wit that is coincidentally reminiscent of the Metaphysicals – on yoking together heterogeneous elements. When the 3-year-old Oskar Matzerath stunts his growth by flinging himself down the steps of the cellar to land head first on the cement floor, the narrative focuses on the odour of raspberry syrup emerging from the bottles he has smashed by pulling a shelf with him (*TD*, p. 58). While the Polish Post Office in Danzig is being shot to pieces by German artillery, and wounded postal officials are dying, Jan Bronski is carefully building a house of cards (*TD*, p. 237). And Grass reminds us of John Donne's poem about the flea which unites the lovers by sucking blood from both when Oskar squashes between his fingers a louse he has just caught on a Russian soldier who is shooting at Matzerath in the Danzig cellar. Matzerath, to conceal his party badge from the Russians, had swallowed it and, suffocating, startled the Russians by thrashing violently about with his arms. Oskar watches the ants, who make a detour around the corpse in their journey towards the sugar which has spilled out of a burst sack (*TD*, pp. 384–7).

Grass is relentless in the pursuit of anomalies, but comes closest to contriving a variation on the marriage between the puppet and the ballerina when Herbert Truczinski dies while trying to rape a wooden figurehead representing Niobe. He is working as an attendant in the Maritime Museum and, despite the shortness of her thighs, the wooden Niobe is irresistibly beautiful. Unable to penetrate her, he has lustfully impaled himself and her on a double-headed axe. 'Up top, then, they were perfectly united, but down below, alas, he had found no ground for his anchor and his member still emerged, stiff and perplexed, from his open trousers' (*TD*, p. 190). Grass has evolved the incident in much the same way as he evolved the idea of Oskar's glass-shattering scream. Other people have described screams as sounding as if they could shatter glass, and Grass had already taken the image one stage further in a poem called 'The School for Tenors', which appeared in his 1956 collection *The Advantages of Windfowl*: the tenor is instructed to puff out his chest, wait until the lady's attention has wandered and then, finally, sing 'the note which glasses fear' (*GG*, p. 30). No one else could have dramatized the image as Grass does in the novel. In letting the wooden Niobe kill Herbert Truczinski, what he was dramatizing was his own image – inspired by Kleist – about the marriage between the puppet and the ballerina: the imagination that formed the phrase would later come surprisingly close to making two characters consummate the union. The resonance of the incident also depends on its relevance to what the artist is always doing – forcing himself on material that may seem dangerously unyielding. Grass is at his best when expanding a Metaphysical conceit into a parable of his own experience.

2

WINDFOWLS AND TALKING RATS

'Everything I've so far written', said Grass during an interview in 1970, 'has its origin and impulse in the lyrical.'[8] The best introduction to the workings of his imagination is provided by the early poems and drawings, but the English reader, unless he understands German, has to make do with an inadequate selection of poems. The anonymous editor of *Selected Poems* (1966) has included only fourteen of the forty-four poems in his first volume, *The Advantages of Windfowl* (1956) and only fourteen of the sixty-four in his second, *Gleisdreieck* (1960). (Gleisdreieck is the name of an underground station near the Berlin Wall.) The volume *In the Egg and Other Poems* (1978) reprints these twenty-eight poems together with twenty-seven from the forty-three in his 1967 volume *Ausgefragt* (*Thoroughly Examined*).

What is most remarkable about these early poems is the way Grass, like a cook who delights in unorthodox combinations, mixes pungently contrasted subject matter.

> Slowly the football went up into the sky.
> Now you could see the grandstand was full.
> Alone the poet stood in the goal,
> but the referee whistled: Offside. (*GG*, p. 54)

This succinct poem is titled 'Stadium at Night', and the movement from the first line to the second associates the football, which is presumably white, with the moon which might have illuminated the spectators. The poet is a game-player, alone on the defensive, but the game is interrupted by a higher authority. It is uncertain whether it is the poet or one of the attacking forwards who is judged to be illicitly between the ball and the opponents' goal. In any case the ball, which has risen, is out of play. While the language is simple and precise, the statement is full of resonant ambiguities.

Though he has learnt from the Symbolists, the Expressionists and the Surrealists, Grass's confident idiosyncrasies are his own, while many of the images which recur, almost obsessively, in the early poems, drawings and plays will recur in the fiction – nuns, scarecrows, snails, eels, teeth. *Dog Years* develops the association between teeth and the Nazi persecution of the Jews; dental decay is associated with German national guilt in the poem 'Small Summons to the Big Mouth-opening or the Gargoyle Speaks'. Mouth-opening is equated with confession, which is the only way to get rid of the decay that has survived for a long time, underneath the toothpaste. We must give up

> the bad gold teeth
> which we broke and plucked from the dead.

Now that we are fathers ourselves, and putting on weight, we must vomit up our guilty parents, and we cannot do this without opening our mouths (*GG*, p. 142). The poem hinges on the association between opening the mouth in the dentist's chair and opening the mouth to confess, while the gold teeth suggest the gold salvaged from the mouths of Jews gassed in concentration camps. In *Dog Years* the structure of associations will be much more complex. In his novels and plays, as in his verse, Grass allows free play to his fantasy and, as in the story of Herbert Truczinski's attempt to rape the wooden figurehead or Oskar Matzerath's awareness of the raspberry syrup, the narrative line will be shaped around a Metaphysical conceit or a poetic association. Many of Grass's effects depend on making a simile into a metaphor and then dramatizing it.

The white football is like a moon; the football rises slowly in the sky.

In another poem, instead of mentioning mothballs by name, he speaks of white balls asleep in the pockets of old clothes, dreaming about moths. A flower-patterned silk dress is described like this:

> Aching silk
> asters and other inflammable flowers
> autumn which becomes a dress. (*GG*, p. 24)

A poem describing a concert in the open air, a conflict between instruments and birds, culminates in the conductor's shooting all the blackbirds with an airgun (*GG*, p. 32). Blissful ignorance of the way politics can interfere with tranquil domesticity is compared with sleeping in a trumpet and assuming it will never be blown (*GG*, p. 74). A similar sense of precariousness informs the poem 'In the Egg'. Living in it, we scribble indecent drawings on the inside of the shell. Assuming that a benevolent fowl is hatching us, we speculate about its colour and breed, but it is possible that the shell will never break, or that it will be cracked just above a frying pan by someone who is hungry (*GG*, pp. 101–2).

Some of the poems hint at an ascetic aesthetic programme. In 'Abstinence', the cat, who is giving all the orders, tells the artist to use a sharp-pointed pencil (which is grey) to shade in brides and snow (which are both white).

> Thou shalt love the colour grey . . . (*GG*, p. 118)

We are reminded of Krudewil's grey wool. The poet is ordered never to wear a new suit, but to dress in the evening paper. He must scatter ash on the geraniums, and avoid cherries, poppies and nosebleed. He must even write the word 'Abstinence' with his sharp pencil over the green in the picture on the wall. This comically strict rejection of colour has a great deal to do with the media Grass has chosen to work in as an artist – in the catalogue for a 1978 exhibition of his drawings, etchings and lithographs at the Patrick Seale Gallery in London, he wrote: 'I have little sense of colour: the scale between black and white is enough for me. As soon as I grow confident in one medium I move on, from ink to lead, to charcoal.'

There are also programmatic hints in the poem 'Diana – or the Objects', though the goddess is more huntress than muse. She aims at his soul, which to her is an object; the missile which hits it is an object; the goddess is herself objective. He has never let his body, which casts shadows, be hurt by an idea, which casts none (*GG*, p. 133). The advice to be inferred is that only objects are to be trusted, and like his prose, his verse has its texture thickened by incessant reference to solid things.

Often he finds it easier to realize the solidity of the object by taking it away from the context in which we usually see it. A Gothic cathedral collides with an American aircraft-carrier in mid-Pacific (*GG*, p. 108). The moon can be rubbed out with a duster on the blackboard sky (*GG*, p. 29). A toad sits on a gasometer (*GG*, p. 47). The piano is in the zoo (*GG*, p. 53).

Noah's flood appeals to Grass as a theme partly as an image of cataclysmic disaster, partly because objects float away from the places where they are normally seen.

> We're waiting for the rain to stop,
> though we've got used to standing
> behind the curtain, to being invisible.
> Spoons are now sieves, people no longer dare
> to reach a hand out.
> Swimming in the streets now are things
> which in dry times were properly concealed.
> Embarrassing to see neighbours' worn out beds.
> We stare at the water-gauge
> comparing worries like watches.
> Much can be regulated.
> But when reservoirs run over, the inherited cup is full
> we'll have to pray
> The cellar is flooded, we've brought the crates up
> and we're checking contents against the inventory.
> Up to now, nothing's been lost. –

Since the flood can't last much longer
we've begun to sew parasols.
It will be very hard to walk across the square again,
clear-cut, shadow heavy as lead.
At first we'll miss the curtain
and often go down to the cellar
to gaze at the mark
the water left us. (*GG*, p. 25)

This might seem like highly unpromising material for the theatre, but Grass made it into his first full-length play, *Flood*, written in 1955 and staged by Frankfurt students in 1957. The talking rats on the roof come from another poem, 'Saturn', in which rats 'know about the drainage' (*GG*, p. 151). The set shows the house in cross-section, from the flat roof to the cellar stairs, which are littered with objects – candelabra, photograph albums, loose photographs. Noah and Betty, his sister-in-law, are trying to move a heavy crate up the stairs. He wants to save his collection of inkwells and candelabra; she is more interested in the photographs, souvenirs of the past. In the room above, the space (as in Ionesco's 1955 play *The New Tenant*) is almost entirely taken up by objects – grandfather clock, bourgeois furniture, crates, candelabra, photograph albums. In the space that is still clear, Noah's daughter, Yetta, is sitting on a bed with her boyfriend, Henry. Through the window she can look out at the beds which are floating past:

Empty, vacated beds. I wish I could be a bed like that, empty, tossing about. Not standing on four legs, under an idiotic oil painting, tied to the chamber pot and the bedside table, false teeth in glass of water, detective story with bookmark, dreaming the murder to the bitter end, and putting up with the seventy years that some people spend on earth from sheer habit. Maybe I'd drift into the woods, but first I'd shake off the pillow. (*FP*, p. 36)

The movement of the free-associating prose is like the movement of a Grass poem. Betty sews parasols in preparation for the return of sunny weather. There is little action: as in the poem 'Flood', Grass's main interest seems to be in displacing objects from their usual position, and in showing how easily people accommodate themselves to catastrophe, how hard it is for them to welcome the return of normality. At the end of the play Yetta is longing for the floodwater to return.

Though the word 'flood' is not mentioned, we will be reminded of both poem and play in *The Tin Drum* when the dangerous wooden woman is

> sealed up in the cellar of the museum, allegedly to be restored, preserved in any case. But you can't lock up disaster in a cellar. It drains into the sewer pipes, spreads to the gas pipes, and gets into every household with the gas. And no one who sets his soup kettle on the bluish flames suspects that disaster is bringing his supper to a boil. (*TD*, p. 191)

The gas cannot fail to stir memories of concentration camps.

The prose in Grass's novels is the prose of a poet who is no more interested in plot than in resonance, no more interested in the story he's telling than in the history behind it. His habit in putting words together is to generate tension by making connections between disparate areas of subject matter. He is good at bringing characters to life, but the flow of energy is so prodigious that the prose receptacle would overflow if he did not move freely and frequently between foreground and background, past and present, first person and third, objectivity and subjectivity. At its best, his prose has an exciting richness of texture, and in the first two-thirds of *The Tin Drum*, as in the first half of *Dog Years*, it is nearly always at its best.

3

DRUMS AND EELS

Though Grass has no obvious affinity with Mark Twain, the creativity of both men erupted into a ferocious rejection of the values they had been educated to accept. Twain's child-based counterworld – like his rejection of his baptismal name, Samuel Clemens – was born from his desperate urge to dissociate himself from the Virginian parents who took pride in a family tree that rooted them into the slave-owning aristocracy. Like Tom Sawyer, Oskar Matzerath will not be allowed to 'drift into manhood'; when Huckleberry Finn drifts down the Mississippi he is in a space that belongs to none of the corrupt adult cultures. A raft is a haven of freedom from interference, a space where friendship can flourish between a boy and a runaway slave.

A rebellious style of writing indicates a rebellious way of finding one's bearings: 'Jim knowed all kinds of signs.' Grass's style and imagery could scarcely be more different from Twain's, but *The Tin Drum* is a story about a boy's way of achieving independence from the adults by finding his own bearings. Together with his size, his intelligence and his willpower, Oskar's magical, glass-shattering scream empowers him to hold the adult world at bay but, unlike Huckleberry Finn, he cannot escape into a zone of freedom: his anarchic counterworld has to be kept alive inside the 'Free City of Danzig' while its freedom is rapidly disappearing. But Oskar's freedom increases as he loses, one by one, his mother and his two presumptive fathers, though the second is not lost until after he has been used in one of Oskar's most grotesque assertions of his freedom. While making love to Maria, Oskar's former girlfriend, Matzerath promises to be particularly careful, but when he tries to withdraw, he finds that he can't. Oskar is on top of him, and the tin drum, which has been plunked down on the small of his back, is being beaten to a rhythm calculated to distract Oskar from the monotonous sounds Maria is uttering and her even more monotonous appeals for her lover's withdrawal. Having escaped the mercy-killing to which Matzerath had consented – Oskar could have been exterminated by the Nazis as abnormal – he uses his father to impregnate his former girlfriend, and goes on to regard the child she bears as his son.

It is no accident that teachers bulk so large in Grass's fiction or that the teachers are such an unsavoury bunch. At the Pestalozzi School Miss Spollenhauer has bobbed hair, a bilious complexion and a 'mincing high-pitched voice'. When she tries to take Oskar's drum away, he uses his scream to attack first her spectacles and then the windows of the classroom (*TD*, pp. 74–8). He is eventually sent to learn his alphabet from Gretchen Scheffler in an overheated room full of dolls and knitting; the cupboards and chests of drawers are packed with baby clothes (*TD*, pp. 84–5). In *Cat and Mouse* (1961) and in *Dog Years* (1963) the teachers who have power are dedicated Nazis, concerned primarily with indoctrinating their pupils; the liberal-minded teachers fall victim to the system.

But in all three fictions the central characters are young boys when the story starts and men when it ends: inevitably, therefore, the process of learning is crucial as it had been in the traditional *Bildungsroman*, which had been a celebration of maturity, bringing the hero to it through a series of enlightening adventures. Finally, as a responsible adult, he was worthy to take his place in society. But what if society was unworthy? Thomas Mann, after ironizing the tradition in *The Magic*

Mountain (1924), which made sickness into a norm while introducing a series of unreliable mentors, went on in *Doctor Faustus* (1949) to deal more directly with the degeneracy of German society, and in his final, unfinished novel, *Confessions of Felix Krull, Confidence Man*, he skittishly charts the progress of a good-looking young man whose adventures, instead of refining his moral scruples, refine his talent for exploiting those who succumb to his good looks.

Whereas Mann's development as a novelist was shaped by growing disillusionment with Germany from the 1920s onwards, Grass's novelistic creativity seems to have its main source in a single surge of disillusionment with all the values he had been educated to accept and with all the adults he had emulated. In 1956, when he left Germany to settle in Paris, he started work on *The Tin Drum* without knowing whether it was going to be a novel or a play. The need to construct a counterworld was so strong that he went on to gamble four years of his life on a book that might, so far as he knew, never have found a publisher.

Unlike Thomas Mann's approach to the novel, Grass's was not primarily literary. He was not trying either to parody the *Bildungsroman* tradition or to invert it but to dispense with it. If the testimony of the untrustworthy narrator – he is a patient in a mental home – is accurate, Oskar starts life with a precocious knowingness:

> The moment I was born I took a very critical attitude towards the first utterances to slip from my parents beneath the light bulbs. My ears were keenly alert. It seems pretty well established that they were small, bent over, gummed up, and in any case cute, yet they caught the words that were my first impressions and as such have preserved their importance for me. And what my ear took in my tiny brain evaluated. After meditating at some length on what I had heard, I decided to do certain things and on no account to do certain others. (*TD*, pp. 42–3)

Disillusioned from the outset, he will not make progress by

shedding illusions; on the other hand, he has plenty to learn, and if the teachers are useless, other sources of information are available. Oskar learns little from his mother, the beautiful Agnes, but her Polish cousin and lover, Jan Bronski, talks informatively about Poland, and he learns about sex from experiences with several women – one a midget and the others fully grown. Another midget, Bebra, an acrobatic musical clown who is often described as Oskar's 'master', is the most useful of his mentors, but he will prove corruptible and unreliable. Generally Oskar does well to distrust his seniors, while trusting his own anarchic instincts. Like the first clown Grass created – Conelli in the play *Rocking Back and Forth* – Oskar knows instinctively about the corruption that has pervaded the world of what looks like adult common sense. Refusing to trust the people who seem to be behaving responsibly, they remain intact by clinging, clownishly, to immaturity. In characterizing Oskar, as in characterizing Mahlke in *Cat and Mouse*, Grass, though he is giving us neither a hero nor a clown, needs to keep taking bearings from both these figures and from Jesus Christ. After being reared between the Holy Ghost and Hitler's photograph, he needed to take a fresh look at the religious images which had been contaminated by association with Nazism. Grass wanted what he makes Oskar want: that other people should get to know themselves through him (*TD*, p. 11).

In beating his tin drum, Oskar is doing roughly what Conelli did on his rocking horse – clinging stubbornly to a symbol of childhood and to a rhythm which might seem meaningless. For Oskar – as perhaps for Grass when he was playing in the jazz band – the meaning of the drumbeats varies according to what is going on in his mind. He might be trying to reconstitute the past or trying to work a spell on the future.

Condemning the first four partitions of Poland they are busily planning a fifth; in the meantime flying to Warsaw via Air France in order to deposit, with appropriate remorse, a wreath on the spot that was once the ghetto. One of these days they will go searching for Poland with rockets. I, meanwhile, conjure up Poland on my drum. And this is what I drum: Poland's lost, but not forever, all's lost, but not forever, Poland's not lost forever. (*TD*, p. 103)

Bebra is first encountered at a circus, where he plays 'Jimmy the Tiger' on bottles and directs a group of Lilliputians. 'Our kind has no place in the audience,' he tells Oskar. 'We must perform, we must run the show. If we don't it's the others that run us' (*TD*, pp. 109–10). The advice he goes on to give will turn out to be important: 'Always take care to be sitting on the rostrum and never to be standing out in front of it. . . . And if not on it, then under it, but never out in front ' (*TD*, p. 110).

At Oskar's next meeting with Bebra, the clown image is developed with specific reference to painting. Now courting favour with Goebbels and Goering, Bebra tries to defend his opportunism by speaking of 'inward emigration'. The allusion here is to the claim made by such writers as Ernest Jünger and Gottfried Benn that it was possible to preserve detachment while remaining in Nazi Germany. Bebra also speaks of the influence wielded by medieval court jesters. He even shows Oskar reproductions of Spanish paintings with midget jesters sporting a goatee beard and wearing a ruff and pantaloons (*TD*, p. 301).

Simultaneously Grass has been charting Oskar's position in relation to Jesus. When Agnes takes her diminutive son to the Church of the Sacred Heart, he sees three coloured plaster sculptures, and in one of them Christ is depicted as a pink, naked 3-year-old. Except for its corkscrew curls, everything about the statue – even its genitals – reminds Oskar of himself.

He had my stature and exactly my watering can, in those days employed exclusively as a watering can. He looked out into the world with my cobalt blue Bronski eyes and – this was what I resented most – he had my very own gestures. When Oskar felt the boy Jesus's watering can, which should have been circumcised but wasn't, when he stroked it and cautiously pressed it as though to move it, he felt a pleasant but strangely new and disturbing sensation in his own watering can, whereupon he left Jesus's alone in the hope that Jesus would let his alone. (*TD*, p. 136)

The Jesus theme is memorably resumed when Oskar becomes the leader of a gang, the Dusters, who ransack churches. When they vandalize the Church of the Sacred Heart, it takes them forty minutes to saw off the infant Jesus from the Virgin's lap. After being lifted up to fill the empty space, Oskar is worshipped in a parodic mass, and during the Kyrie he beats his tin drum (*TD*, p. 372). Later on, when he is working as a model for an eccentric post-surrealist painter, he is armed with a pistol to pose as Jesus taking aim at the Madonna. He is also painted as Jesus the drummer boy, sitting on the lap of a sexually excited 'Madonna 49' (*TD*, pp. 464–5).

Grass's plotting seems to be shaped partly by the need to provide himself with pretexts for verbal paintings of scenes in which either an artist is creating an image or a character is measuring himself against an archetype. Grass needs to compare Oskar not only with Jesus but also with the classical hero. Returning to Danzig after his adventures in Berlin, Oskar insists that he is not like Ulysses at the moment of returning to Penelope, but more like the Prodigal Son (*TD*, p. 339); later the painter makes him into a humpbacked Ulysses (*TD*, p. 491). To clarify his own image of Oskar as the character develops, Grass needs these points of reference. Though he does not refer explicitly to the handsome, Nordic, patriotic heroes of the fiction that had served as Nazi propaganda, Grass was reacting robustly against this phoney stereotype by offering a spirited little monster as an alternative.

Grass's points of reference derive principally from his training in the visual arts. His fiction is visibly influenced by the German Expressionists and by painters of the *Neue Sachlichkeit* (New Objectivity). German Expressionism, which began as a revolt against the colourful hedonism of French

Impressionism and landscape painting, cultivated primitivism while reviving the rough, jagged stylization of medieval German woodcuts. The *Neue Sachlichkeit* had some of its roots in Dada subversiveness, but it emphasized the need for fidelity to tangible reality. Its outstanding exponents were Otto Dix, who made violent statements about the ugliness of psychological experience, and Georg Grosz, whose social satire bordered on a nightmarish vision of bourgeois bestiality. Like Döblin, he exerted a direct influence on Brecht, who (together with Döblin) influenced Grass. Grass was also influenced, as Brecht had been, by Grimmelshausen's fiction of 1669, *Der Abenteureliche Simplicissimus Teutsch*. Set during the Thirty Years War, it is a grotesque and partly comic narrative about the adventures of a boy who is brought up on the farm of his putative father, and subsequently educated by his real father, without knowing who he is. After the death of the real father, a hermit, he survives an attempt to drive him insane. The book has many themes in common with *The Tin Drum*, which skilfully preserves its ambiguity on the question of whether Oskar is sane. The first sentence is: 'Granted: I am an inmate of a mental hospital; my keeper is watching me, he never lets me out of his sight; there's a peephole in the door, and my keeper's eye is the shade of brown that can never see through a blue-eyed type like me.' This opening is oddly similar to the opening of Saul Bellow's 1961 novel *Herzog*: 'If I am out of my mind, it's all right with me, thought Moses Herzog.' But Grass, unlike Bellow, is suggesting that the narrative is suspect. While we have no problem over whether to believe the third person narrative about Herzog, Oskar's veracity cannot be taken for granted, and when other narrators briefly take over the reins, it confirms that we have reason to be suspicious. Jean-Paul Sartre described Vladimir Nabokov as having the exile's desire to knock down the material he has constructed; Grass, an exile from Danzig, starts to play the Nabokovian game of abandoning the reader to an untrustworthy narrator, a game which will take up more of his energy in *Cat and Mouse* and *Dog Years*.

Pivotal to the success of *The Tin Drum* was Grass's good

fortune in happening on an idea that would make it possible to be extremely funny about Nazi Germany without seeming flippant. The boy who refuses to grow is an image which would probably not have occurred to Grass if he had not been both a sculptor and a poet. When he was about 22, he worked on a long poem about a village bricklayer who gets so fed up with life that he builds himself a tall column in the square. Standing on top of it, he has a different perspective on everything that goes on around him, but he is now just an observer, which makes the narrative so static that Grass abandoned the poem and reversed the idea. The saint-like drop-out, who removes himself to look at society from above, is replaced by a malicious boy, whose intelligence is more developed than his body. He is big enough to peer over the edge of the table and small enough to see underneath it when Agnes, his mother, her German husband and her Polish lover are playing *Skat*, a three-handed card-game. Jan isn't concentrating on the cards. He has slipped off a shoe and Oskar is fascinated to watch a foot in its sock – grey, of course – as it locates Agnes's knee. She moves in closer to the table. After the toe has lifted the hem of her dress, the entire foot disappears under the skirt. Oskar notices, admiringly, that she can still apply her mind to both the card-game and the conversation. A former Catholic, Grass loves triadic forms, and here he is playing with two triangles. Agnes preserves a precarious, almost balletic equilibrium between ardent lover and complaisant husband, while Oskar's dwindling loyalty and growing malevolence will be divided between his two fathers.

Unlike the static bricklayer, he is extremely active. His main weapon is his glass-shattering scream, but he is dangerous in several ways. In presenting a little monster as his hero, Grass is commenting on the ideal of heroism as purveyed by the Third Reich. He was decisively rejecting the handsome, blue-eyed, patriotic heroes of the stories he read during boyhood. Oskar is often destructive and always unpredictable, but however viciously he behaves, our sympathy is never entirely alienated. We might be less tolerant if we were seeing him in a different environment, more like that of England in the eighteenth century or even the 1930s but this is a background in which brutality has been licensed. Cruelty has become the norm. Meyn, the trumpeter who plays sublimely when drunk, is expelled from the SA for his cruelty to cats but commended for his ruthlessness in beating up Jews. Oskar, because he is so diminutive, is a natural victim, and we begin to sympathize when a group of bigger children, led by the merciless Susi Kater, force him to drink an unspeakably filthy 'soup', containing spittle and urine (TD, p. 93). Many of Oskar's most destructive and subversive actions are aimed against an establishment which is being progressively corroded by Nazism. Taking Bebra's advice about the advantages of being under the rostrum, he subverts a parade by hiding under a platform and using his tin drum to beat out a rhythm which not only confuses the drummers of the Young Folk and the Hitler Youth, but also infects the crowd of spectators with an irresistible urge to dance the Charleston to the tune Bebra had played on the bottles – 'Jimmy the Tiger'. Even the hunchbacked Löbsack, the district chief of training, falls under the spell of the drumbeat.

All those who were not yet dancing hastened to snatch up the last available partners. But Löbsack had to dance with his hump, for near him there was not a single member of the fair sex to be had, and the NS [National Socialist] ladies who might have come to his help were far away, fidgeting on the hard wooden benches of the rostrum. Nevertheless – as his hump advised him – he danced, trying to put a good face on the horrible Jimmy music and to save what could still be saved. But the situation was beyond saving. The national comrades danced away from the Maiwiese and soon the grassy field, though badly trampled, was quite deserted. The national comrades had vanished with Jimmy the Tiger in the spacious grounds of the nearby Steffens-Park. There they found the jungle that Jimmy promised; there tigers moved on velvet paws, an ersatz jungle for the sons and daughters of the German nation, who only a short while before had been crowding round the rostrum. Gone were law and order. (*TD*, p. 117)

The rhythm of the prose celebrates the transformation of the parade into a carnival and the reader responds gratefully to Grass's warm-hearted playfulness. The distinctive flavour of *The Tin Drum* results from the combination of cheerful anarchic comedy with a profoundly macabre pessimism. In the tonal dialectic, this dance of the nationalist comrades in the meadow is countered by the morbid sequence in which the central image is the decapitated head of a recently slaughtered horse with a black mane. It is Good Friday. Oskar, Agnes, Jan and Matzerath see an old man fishing in the brackish water of the Mottlau, using a clothes line and no float. Instead of answering when Agnes asks what he's doing, he spits out a long viscous train of tobacco juice, which bobs up and down in the sludge until a circling seagull swoops down to claim it. When the old man pulls his line in, they see the horse's head at the end of it, bait to catch eels. Dragged to the shore, some are seized by gulls, but most are stuffed, wriggling, into a sack where they will squirm to death in the salt. Agnes is violently sick, and the gulls squabble over her regurgitated breakfast.

The unpleasantness of the episode, which might seem gratuitous, is functional. It forces her to a fatal reassessment of the two relationships at the core of her life. At first she shrinks into abstinence, refusing to eat fish or eels; soon, compulsively, self-destructively, she is gorging herself on fish, eating inordinate quantities every day, at all times of the day. She is pregnant, but the child will never be born. She has had enough of life, we are told, especially of men, perhaps also of Oskar. When she is a corpse, her face is described as nauseated.

The narrative of events is highly effective, but the realization of her nausea is more painterly than dramatic, and the episode is illuminated if we look at Grass's drawings. In returning again and again to eels – as he does to snails, fish, mushrooms, nuns, scarecrows – he is fascinated by the indefiniteness of the borderline between human and non-human. In writing, as in the graphic arts, the artist is a god who with pen, pencil, brush or chisel can transform vegetable into animal, animate into inanimate or can create ambiguities. A nexus of lines can represent something which is both human and non-human. In one of the lithographs from Grass's 1976 series *Mushrooming with Sophie*, a sketchy female head is trying to emerge from beneath a mushroom, with a penis tip growing out of its ambiguous stem. Next to it is a similarly tipped mushroom, drawn more sketchily, with a male body vigorously crawling out from underneath, but the hairless male head itself resembles the tip of a penis, while the patches of dark under the arms suggest a tunnel. As in Grass's drawings and engravings of animals (such as eels and snails) which might be reminiscent of the phallus in both appearance and movement, the effect is entirely dry, but there is a moist effluvium when he writes about suction. His sensual imagination infiltrates both the act of looking and the art of recording the vision.

Another reason, suggested in John Reddick's book on Grass,[9] for the fascination eels exert on him, is that, like worms, they eat dead human flesh. Shakespeare makes Hamlet reflect: 'A man may fish with the worm that hath eat of a King and eat of the fish that hath fed of the worm . . . a King may go a progress through the guts of a beggar' (IV. iii. 267). We eat eels which may have fed on human corpses, and after his mother has gorged herself to death, Oskar half expects her to vomit up a bit of an eel which may have fed on the body of her father, Josef Koljaiczek, the arsonist, who possibly drowned under a raft in the Mottlau.

Together with images based on the triadic form, images of circularity are recurrent in *The Tin Drum*. Human existence is a roundabout; God the Father is the vicious owner of a merry-go-round which carries children to their death. Refused admission to a ferry which would take only troops across the Vistula, 4000 children from East Prussia are blown up on a train at Käsemark. After hearing this, Oskar dreams feverishly that he is one of many weeping, dizzy children, clamouring to dismount from the merry-go-round, but the Heavenly Father is standing next to it, and each time it stops, he puts another coin in, treating them to another unwanted ride. They are carried past our Father in heaven, who now has a different face, the face of Rasputin. Then he is Goethe, then Rasputin again (*TD*, pp. 404–5). Another image of circularity occurs in *Cat and Mouse*, where the schoolboys pick seagull excrement off the sides of the boat, chew it as if it were gum, and then spit the slimy residue into the water, where the gulls who greedily pounce on it will eat their own recycled faeces.[10]

Many of the sequences derive their vividness from Grass's feeling for his native Danzig, for its circling seagulls, for the banks of the Vistula, for life in the Kashubian potato fields, for the suburb of Langfuhr, where he grew up. His uncle is now running the grocer's shop, with the staircase leading down to the cellar floor which stunted Oskar's growth, and the present-day visitor to the suburb will still find streets and buildings corresponding to Grass's lively description.[11] Like Joyce, who recreated Dublin while in exile from it, Grass has an almost erotic connection with his native city.

The influence of nativity is not merely scenic. The early sequence set in the muddy Kashubian potato field gives a clear impression of the wind, the brickyard, the telegraph poles, the mole-hills, the furze bordering the sunken lane, the dark boulder at the end of the field, the old woman cooking potatoes over a fire (*TD*, pp. 13–20). As in the urban episodes, the feeling for the setting is the feeling of someone who belongs to it. His mother's family was Kashubian, and he says that when he visited her part of the family he was deeply impressed by the simple way of life, the humour and the optimism. An old Slavic tribe, constantly at risk from the nationalist fanaticism of both Germans and Poles, the Kashubians needed to develop a cynical resourcefulness. Grass tells the story of a cousin whose job it was before 1939 to climb a tree and report whether the Poles or the Germans were coming. The appropriate flag would then be hoisted.[12]

In the face of danger Grass's characters may be preoccupied

with something irrelevant or may be cowardly, but they are never heroic. When the Polish post office is under siege, Jan, who has been ordered to shoot through a space between the sandbags, lifts up his right leg towards it, hoping for a bullet wound. Exhausted from holding this difficult position, he lies on his back, propping up his right leg with his hand, exposing both calf and heel (*TD*, pp. 226–7).

Grass also likes using his metaphysical conceits to trivialize military action by juxtaposing it with comedy or with anomalous incidents. At the meal after the baptism of Kurt, the unwanted child of Matzerath and Maria, the guests argue about U-boats, and one of them, using his left hand to illustrate the movement of a diving submarine, knocks over a glass of beer (*TD*, p. 297). Oskar makes love to the midget Roswitha in a Berlin cellar during a major air raid (*TD*, p. 321); later her death in Normandy is synchronized with the Allied invasion (*TD*, p. 338).

Throughout the novel Grass makes brilliant use of his prodigiously fertile imagination, and if the book deteriorates slightly towards the end, it is because he has set himself an insoluble formal problem. His fundamental concern is with the historical background. Throughout the first two-thirds of the story, the action in the foreground makes so much impact that a balance is maintained. Unlike the hero of the *Bildungsroman*, Oskar is progressing not towards enlightened maturity but towards independence, and so long as he goes on liberating himself from the intrusive claims of his corrupt family and his misleading mentors, the story keeps its momentum. But the deterioration – which is considerably less serious than the deterioration at the end of *Dog Years* – sets in just after two-thirds of the way through the story, when Oskar buries his drum (*TD*, p. 398) and starts to grow again (*TD*, p. 410). Little is gained by making Bruno take over the narration on pages 412–21, and Grass tries in this section to base his perspective partly on the growth of the German Social Democratic Party. When Oskar resumes the story-telling, Grass begins to lean too heavily on autobiography – seeing Gustav Gründgens and

Elisabeth Flickenschildt act in Düsseldorf (*TD*, p. 428), experiences as an apprentice tombstone-maker (*TD*, pp. 430–40). The image of Oskar the hunchback never becomes so vivid as the image of the Oskar who has arrested his growth at the height of 4 feet 1 inch, though the hump is well used in the modelling sequences. The problem of German reunification is badly served by the Metaphysical conceit which links it to a pair of Chinese Lesbians who can't get together (*TD*, p. 461) – Grass is sometimes overconfident about preserving a balance between flippancy and commitment – while the second recapitulation of the story about the horse's head and the eels (*TD*, pp. 487–8) makes less impact than the story did in its first two tellings.

Throughout the first two-thirds of the narrative Grass seldom appears to be recycling his own experience. Even if there is a connection between the 15-year-old boy who still sat on his mother's lap and the boy who chose to stop growing, it is adequately subsumed, but Grass's experiences as a jazz drummer are sometimes filtered too directly into Oskar's adventures, while the post-war background remains stubbornly pallid in comparison with the earlier background, which was treated less satirically. One sign of faltering control over the material is uncertainty about how much recapitulation is necessary. There is, for instance, a superfluous resumé of the main story under pretext of rendering Oskar's wandering thoughts while drumming (*TD*, p. 499).

One of the most telling images in the post-war section is the Onion Cellar, an expensive and fashionable bar, where each of the guests is given an onion to peel. Reduced to tears, the prosperous customers find their way to the confessional candour which is normally so elusive in the Germany of the Economic Miracle. 'Still hesitant, startled by the nakedness of their own words, the weepers poured out their hearts to their neighbours on the uncomfortable, burlap-covered crates, submitted to questioning, let themselves be turned inside-out like overcoats' (*TD*, p. 517). It is in this cellar that the hunchback Oskar reverts to drumming in the manner of his earlier self

(*TD*, p. 525), conjuring up the image of the evil witch, black as pitch, who had frightened him during childhood. (She is a less suggestive figure than her German original, *die schwarze Köchin*, the black cook. In German, the image relates to the humiliating ritual in which bigger children force Oskar to eat the vile 'soup' they have mixed.) The onion peelers react to Oskar's drumming rather like the marchers in the Nazi parade, but the sequence is less successful, partly because Grass has come so close to repeating himself.

Even if Grass's perverse variant on the *Bildungsroman* leaves him with an insoluble formal problem, many of these difficulties would have been obviated if the development of Oskar had been charted over a shorter period and if the story had ended with the end of the war. The decision to continue the narrative seems to have been prompted mainly by the wish to expose the continuity in German life. Like Heinrich Böll, Grass was intensely irked by the amnesia of his compatriots, who wanted to assume that with defeat and constitutional change, the evil had been eradicated, as if by magic. Grass was intent on showing it had not, even if he had to damage his novel in the process.

4

CATS AND DOGS

The looseness of structure in most of Grass's fiction is motivated partly by his need to allow scope for digressions. The one fiction which has none is not a novel: the novella *Cat and Mouse* was published in 1961, though his wall-charts show that some of the material was ready even before he had finished *The Tin Drum*.[13] While preparing to write this novella he made a careful study of the genre;[14] one reason for the inferiority of his later work is that he became more indifferent not only to questions of form but also to the aesthetic programme he had himself formulated. The principle announced in the essay 'Content as Resistance' is 'to sew mistrust between form and content'; nowhere does he achieve this more spectacularly than in *Cat and Mouse*.

The narrator, Pilenz, is unreliable. He contradicts himself frequently, and his memory is inadequate to the task of reconstructing episodes from his life as a schoolboy. It is soon clear that Mahlke is to be the central character, but Pilenz is not even sure about the colour of his eyes. He also appears to be dissimulating about their relationship. Claiming to have been a devoted friend, Pilenz reveals that he was the most dangerous of Mahlke's persecutors. That title of the story points to Mahlke's protuberant Adam's apple, which was active even when he was asleep; it was Pilenz who encouraged the caretaker's young cat, mistaking it for a mouse, to claw it. Gradually the story detaches itself from the narrative: skilfully Grass invites us to make inferences about what happened, levering ourselves away from what Pilenz is telling us.

In his relationship with Mahlke Pilenz seems at first to be motivated by admiration and loyalty, but these positive feelings are poisoned by envy, and his destructiveness is brought brilliantly into focus against a background in which Danzig is succumbing to Nazism and the war. With his prowess as a swimmer Mahlke is the only one of the schoolboys who can dive down to bring up trophies from the sunken Polish minesweeper in the harbour, and he goes on distinguishing himself, in a series of daring feats, which inflame Pilenz's jealousy and vindictiveness. He is the cat and Mahlke the mouse. Guilt feelings are at the root of Pilenz's need to tell the story. The former altar boy has become secretary in a Catholic welfare house. He reads Böll and idly discusses theological questions with an old Franciscan who only half believes. Pilenz can survive in a poisonous atmosphere, but Mahlke, unable to resolve his problems in any other way, dives to an underwater death. Like Böll's series of deserters from the German army, he is rejecting Hitlerism.

Before he could go any further, Grass had to work through this unavoidable concern with conformism and dissidence under Nazism. But – partly because *Cat and Mouse* is more realistic than *The Tin Drum* – Mahlke will have less opportunity than Oskar for deviant behaviour, though, once again, the conception of the central, deviant personality depends on bearings taken from three archetypes – the clown, Jesus Christ and the classical hero. In addition to his outsize Adam's apple, Mahlke has several physical characteristics which are consistent with his professed intention of working as a circus clown when he grows up (*CM*, p. 26). When he looks solemn, people are liable to laugh at his expression; while the other boys go brown in the sun, he goes as red as a lobster (*CM*, p. 17). His spinal column is prominent, the back of his head protrudes, his eyelids are almost lashless, his ears stick out, and his genitals are unusually large. As a cyclist he cuts a ludicrous figure, with his knees going out sideways as he pedals (*CM*, p. 11). When Pilenz sees him in church on the second Sunday of Advent, Mahlke's neck is sprouting from a white Schiller collar, which is sticking out above the reversed and remodelled overcoat he has inherited from his engine-driver father. His muffler is fastened with a large safety-pin (*CM*, p. 128). He parts his hair in the middle, using, instead of hair-cream, sugar dissolved in water; he buys five or six of the luminous badges worn at this time by elderly people to protect them from collisions during blackouts. 'You turned yourself into a clown,' Pilenz comments.

The clowning is a protest against conformism, while the allusions to the Passion make us think of Mahlke as a saviour manqué. He could have done a routine as Jesus on the stage, we are told, and casual phrases drive the point home. After being called up, Mahlke reappears at the school when he has won the Knight's Cross, hoping he will be invited to give a lecture. His hair is no longer parted in the middle: 'the redeemer's hair-do was gone. . . . But the countenance was still that of a redeemer' (*CM*, p. 160).

Where Oskar had refused to grow up into the Third Reich, no such option is open to Mahlke, but we see how he suffers in a society that is inimical to humane impulses. We never learn what he would have said in his lecture to his old school, but we guess that it would have been a counterblast to the jingoistic lectures he'd been obliged, earlier in the war, to hear. After the talk by the lieutenant, Mahlke is the only schoolboy not to applaud (*CM*, p. 72). After the talk by the lieutenant-commander, it is found that his medal has disappeared: Mahlke has stolen it. The headmaster who expels him, Dr Klohse, is a high-ranking Party official, who will remain hostile, even after Mahlke has won a medal of his own. It is after being refused permission to lecture that Mahlke will embark on the series of decisions that lead to his disappearance. Almost certainly he is dead. As Grass has said in an interview, 'His downfall exposes church, school, the hero-business — all of society. In his failure is the failure of everything.'[15]

*

Like James Joyce, who while living in Paris lovingly reconstructed Dublin in *Ulysses*, Grass did the bulk of his best writing about Danzig while living outside Germany. In Paris during the period 1956–60, he cooked up a mass of material without knowing what form it would take when it came out of the stockpot.[16] According to John Reddick, who has had access to the wall plans Grass made for *Dog Years*, *Cat and Mouse* was conceived as integral to this novel, while the images of the ice warehouse and the mound of bones (which are both important in *Dog Years*) were originally intended for *The Tin Drum*. The two novels and the novella overlap: several of the characters are mentioned in two or all three of them, while the Polish minesweeper lying on the sea-bed in the harbour, which is mentioned briefly in *Dog Years* (p. 269), is central in *Cat and Mouse*: the boys repeatedly dive down to plunder it. In both novels, too, wartime schoolboys are subjected to militaristic speeches given by wounded veterans. In *Cat and Mouse* the treacherous Pilenz throws Mahlke's tin-opener into the sea; in *Dog Years* the incident is echoed when the treacherous Walter Matern throws into the Vistula the pocket-knife which had once shed his blood, together with Eddie Amsel's when, at the age of 8, they took an oath of blood brotherhood.

Both fictions start out from a close friendship in which subservience and emotional dependence will give way to vicious hostility. Unlike Matern's perfidy, Pilenz's, though seen against a background of debased values, has no direct connection with Nazism. Amsel is half-Jewish, and Matern is one of nine masked thugs who beat him up, knocking out all his teeth. Here, as in the poem 'Small Summons to the Great Mouth-Opening', knocked-out teeth call up memories of concentration camps.

Unlike Pilenz and Mahlke, Matern and Amsel are both artists. Matern is a second-rate actor; Amsel is highly talented. He starts out as a maker of scarecrows and ends up as a ballet-master and choreographer. Like Pempelfort and Krudewil, Matern and Amsel represent inferior and superior artistry. While the second-rater is a romantic, incapable of looking reality in its grey face, the good artist is a realist, and while second-rate art is not inimical to Nazism, the novel implies that good art is, just as Nazism is inimical to good art. When he paints the huge, black, aggressive German Shepherd dog, Harras, who has come to symbolize Nazi brutality, Amsel seems to be taming – and therefore 'ruining' – the dog. Though Harras never attacks him, a little encouragement from the fascistic girl Tulla Pokriefke is enough to make Harras attack the inoffensive music teacher, Felsner-Imbs, three times. The carpenter Matern, father of Walter and owner of Harras, says: 'I'm sure he doesn't think much of artists' (*DY*, p. 162).

The scarecrows – figures which appear to dance in the wind – may be descended from Kleist's essay on the puppets, and from Grass's attempt to consummate the ballerina's marriage with the puppet in the business of the figurehead in *The Tin Drum*. We are reminded of this when Amsel experiments in 'mating human and tree' (*DY*, p. 48). He constructs a scarecrow modelled partly on a three-headed willow tree and partly on the ferocious Grandmother Matern, who beats her maid with a hardwood cooking spoon (*DY*, p. 20). The hybrid scarecrow scares not only birds, but also horses, cows and even the maid (*DY*, p. 48).

Having established Amsel's artistry by characterizing him as someone who assembles miscellaneous clothes and objects for use in the construction of scarecrows, Grass shows how natural it is for the artist to make statements about the violence he witnesses. When a squad of uniformed Hitler Cubs carry their 'war games' into the Amsels' garden, Matern, still trying to defend his friend, fights with the platoon leader, and Amsel, who has been watching, sketches his observations and builds

> models the size of upright cigar boxes: wrestling groups, a muddled shapeless free-for-all of scrawny Cubs, short-panted, knee-socked, shoulder-strapped, brown-tattered, pennant-maddened, rune-bepatched, dagger belts askew, Führer-vaccinated and hoarse with triumph – the living image of our Cub squad fighting over the pennant in Amsel's garden. Amsel had found his way back to reality; from that

day on he stopped wasting his talent on fashion plates, hothouse plants, studio art; avid with curiosity, he went out into the street. (*DY*, p. 188)

He also begins to construct uniformed scarecrows. In the shops uniforms can be bought only on presentation of a Party card, and Amsel cannot join the Party, but after Matern has joined to overcome this difficulty, Amsel constructs uniformed scarecrows who, with the aid of a mechanism in their stomachs, can march and salute. Grass has found an image for the dehumanizing effect of Nazi uniform: the puppet and the ballerina have spawned robots. This suggestion works alongside the dog imagery, which (like Ionesco's image of the rhinoceros) implies that Nazism is bestializing human nature. Later, as a choreographer, Amsel will incorporate scarecrows into a ballet. The scarecrow image makes yet another appearance in the post-war section of the novel when Matern, travelling by train through western Germany looks out of the window, associating scarecrows with refugees from the eastern zone.

Functionally dressed hatracks leave salad beds and knee-high wheat. Beanpoles buttoned up for winter start and take hurdles. What a moment before was blessing gooseberries with wide-sleeved arms, says amen and trots off. But it's not a flight, more like a relay race. It's not as if they were all hightailing it eastward to the Peace-loving Camp; no, their purpose is to pass something on over here, some news or a watchword; for scarecrows uproot themselves from their vegetable gardens, hand on the baton with the terrible message rolled in it, to other scarecrows who have hitherto been guarding rye, and as the vegetable scarecrows are catching their breath in rye, the rye scarecrows sprint beside the interzonal train until, in a good stand of barley, they encounter scarecrows ready to start, who take over the spook post, relieve breathless rye scarecrows, and with bold checks and beanpole joints keep pace with the on-schedule train, until once again herringbone-patterned rye scarecrows take over. (*DY*, pp. 509–10)

49

In passages such as this Grass's method is much the same as in the verse which brackets together disparate subject-matter.

Whereas Amsel, like Krudewil, bases his art on what he sees in the streets, Matern, like Pempelfort, is likely to misinterpret reality or let himself be distracted from it. In the childhood section Matern, like Pilenz, is nearly always in the subordinate position, a willing adjutant to his more imaginative friend. As an actor, Matern begins as a walk-on and later settles for any role that is offered to him: he is content to play a talking reindeer in *The Snow Queen*. He lacks the talent which enables Amsel to excel in any art – even singing – and above all he lacks Amsel's irony. Amsel can joke even when threatened with violence. Surrounded by nine masked boys who have climbed over the fence of his garden, obviously intending to beat him up, he offers to regale them with coffee and cake, offers to tell them a story (*DY*, pp. 211–12). Unable to sublimate his aggressions into humour, Matern releases them in thuggery. As a child he had practised for the game of *Schlagball* by hitting frogs with his bat (*DY*, p. 99); now, resentfully conscious of his inferiority to Amsel, he goes on punching his friend in the mouth long after the other masked attackers have stopped (*DY*, p. 213). Later, praying to the Virgin Mary and trying to justify the brutality, he says: 'Now tell me, could I help it, it was that cynical streak I couldn't stomach: nothing was sacred to him. That's why. Actually we only wanted to teach him a little lesson' (*DY*, p. 239). In *The Tin Drum* Grass had found himself contriving situations involving a series of artists and pseudo-artists so that he could incorporate statements of his aesthetic principles; in *Dog Years* he is more sophisticated: central to the development of the Amsel-Matern relationship is an exploration of two artistic standpoints.

Even in his acts of contrition, Matern is unsubtle, humourless and aggressive. After calling his father's German Shepherd Dog a Nazi (*DY*, p. 242) he kills the animal with poisoned meat (*DY*, p. 247). While Matern is lumbered with an identity he can never escape, Amsel, as a consummate artist, has protean powers which verge on the magical; even victimization works

50

to his advantage. Eddie Amsel has always been plump, but it is a slim lightfooted young man who arrives in Berlin with a forged passport giving him the name Hermann Haseloff (*DY*, p. 222), and there, at a dental clinic, he has his toothless mouth furnished with thirty-two gold teeth. Soon he will be given the nickname Goldmouth, and his new identity will bring him success in a more glamorous and lucrative career.

The other plump character who is magically slimmed by victimization is Jenny, a ballet student, who is consistently and ruthlessly persecuted by the mean-minded Tulla and other children. The persecution culminates when Jenny, forced to dance in the snow around the Gutenberg monument, keeps falling over; covered in snow, she is helpless as Tulla rolls her over, making her first into a giant snowball and then into a snowman (*DY*, p. 213). But Jenny, saved by her fluffy coat and the thaw which sets in the same evening, emerges from her ordeal with an improved technique as a dancer: she can now do pirouettes (*DY*, p. 222).

In the novel, as in the poems, anything can happen. If Oskar, in stunting his growth, was rejecting the established world of the adults, Grass is stylistically making the same gesture. Neither conventional reality nor conventional realism can be allowed to hold him back. Nor can plot or structure. In *Cat and Mouse* the foreground action had brought the historical background into focus, but Grass has never since filtered so much of his message through a personal relationship. He likes to paint a big historical backdrop and to fabricate myths or cantilever out into different zones of experience. In *Dog Years* he does not make as much use as he had in *The Tin Drum* of Metaphysical conceits; he rarely synchronizes trivial events with historical crises, does not watch a column of ants detouring to avoid a corpse. But he still tests the strength of his glue by the heterogeneity of the materials it can bond together: scarecrows and stormtroopers, black dogs and Nazis.

Like *The Tin Drum*, *Dog Years* deteriorates towards the end, but this time the deterioration is more damaging. Many critics have analysed it – none more cogently than John

Reddick, who finds that the novel 'carries conviction in a masterly way' so long as 'the fiction is detached in time, strongly localised (Schiewenhorst, Nickelswalde and the Vistula, and later Danzig), and clearly structured in terms of character and plot', but he finds the story 'jerky and laboured and persistently unconvincing' in the final two-fifths of its 560 pages. He blames the deterioration on Grass's 'social and political moralism': his 'intense involvement in the state and future of his country' stopped him from being sufficiently detached. Like the scarecrows Amsel produces when, in adult life, he goes back to the art he had abandoned in childhood, Grass's inventions in the later parts of the book are '*Atelier-pflanzen*' – studio plants (*DY*, p. 188) – forced and artificial products.[17]

In my view the deterioration sets in earlier – towards the end of the novel's first half, when a large-scale campaign against Heidegger is launched. It is understandable that Grass should feel hostile to the philosopher, who stayed in Germany and never spoke out decisively against the Nazis. It could be argued that both Heidegger's abstraction and his jargon are motivated by the need to sidestep concrete social and political realities, but it is absurd to hold him responsible for what the Nazis did; though Grass never advances this argument explicitly, he unbalances his novel by introducing a great deal of irrelevant parody, often making characters lapse implausibly into Heideggerian jargon. In May 1938 Matern wanders around the docks quoting Heidegger, together with Gottfried Benn (*DY*, p. 237). When Störtebeker, the former leader of the 'Dusters', becomes an Air Force auxiliary, he talks about 'essents' and calls underdone potatoes 'spuds forgetful of Being' (*DY*, p. 297). When he joins in rat-hunts, he theorizes: 'The rat withdraws itself by unconcealing itself into the ratty. So the rat errates the ratty, illuminating it with errancy. For the ratty has come-to-be in the errancy where the rat errs and so fosters error. That is the essential area of all history' (*DY*, p. 303). Heidegger is one of the models which help Tulla's cousin, Harry Liebenau, to rationalize the slaughter in the concentration camps. 'The pile of bones, which in reality cried out to high heaven between Troyl and Kaiserhafen, was mentioned in his diary as a place of sacrifice, erected in order that purity might come-to-be in the luminous, which transluminates purity and so fosters light' (*DY*, p. 311). Even when Tulla gives premature birth to a foetus after jumping off a bus, the commentary, ostensibly written by Harry, slips into the jargon:

> Ah, are we ourselves ever, is mine ever, now under the leaves, in the ground, not deeply frozen; for higher than reality is potentiality: here manifested: what primarily and ordinarily does not show itself, what is hidden but at the same time is an essential part of what does primarily and ordinarily show itself, namely, its meaning and ground, which is not frozen but loosened with heels of shoes from the Air Force supply room, in order that the baby may come into its there. (*DY*, p. 319)

After experimenting in *The Tin Drum* with an unreliable narrator, and managing in *Cat and Mouse* to make us detach the story from Pilenz's misleading narrative, Grass is still more ambitious in *Dog Years*, dividing the story between three narrators, who contradict each other. The first is Amsel, but as he is writing under one of his pseudonyms, Brauchsel, and refers to himself in the third person, we do not identify him until later. The second is Harry, and the third Matern, who pretentiously uses the title Materniads for an account of his adventures – as a self-appointed avenger, apparently determined to punish acquaintances guilty of brutality during the Nazi period. In practice Matern is easily distracted. Instead of punishing Jochen Sawatzki, formerly a fanatical leader of an SA Sturm, Matern ends up having triangular sex with him and his wife, Inge.

Though it would obviously have been less damaging if Grass could have vented his spleen against Heidegger by letting only one of the three narrators lapse into the jargon, the theme is resumed here, when Inge, a most improbable convert, tries to learn the vocabulary from Matern:

Ingemouse loves it when, snapping snowflakes, he roars, grinds, hisses, and squeezes out strange words: 'I exist self-grounded! World never is, but worldeth. Freedom is freedom to the I. I essent. The projecting I as projecting midst. I, localized and encompassed. I, world-project! I, source of grounding! I, possibility – soil – identification! I, GROUND, GROUNDING IN THE GROUNDLESS!' (*DY*, p. 377)

Later on Matern will tell the dog that Heidegger and Hitler, who were both born in the same year, 1889, will stand on the same pedestal (*DY*, p. 392). Generally the complications involved in using three narrators could be worthwhile if the contradictions were contrived to balance and enrich the narrative, but this does not happen. In the final section of the book, the main focus is meant to come conclusively to rest on Matern's capacity for self-deception, so more is lost than gained by having him tell the story, whereas, in the first section, where Amsel's clarity of vision needs to be established, he is not the ideal narrator, even when writing pseudonymously.

Much of the material used in *Dog Years* derives from a novel which Grass abandoned after writing 350 pages under the title 'Potato Peelings'; the narrator was a maid who had to peel potatoes. It is always hard to mix old material with new and, even with a single narrator, it would have been difficult to achieve unity between the Danzig section of *Dog Years* and the post-war section. It is odd that Grass expected it to be easier with three.

Nevertheless, in spite of all its flaws, *Dog Years* remains one of the most outstanding post-war German novels, second only to *The Tin Drum*. Though Grass no longer has such a dynamic central image, the relationship between Amsel and Matern serves him well and, approaching the Third Reich less obliquely than he did in the earlier novel, he succeeds remarkably well in combining incidents which are representative of Nazi psychology – Tulla's persecution of Jenny, for instance – with poetic images which are representative in a different way. The symbolism of the malevolent black dog works powerfully, while the carnage of the concentration camps is evoked by the mountain of human bones between the city and the asylum at Stutthof. The ambivalent complicity of the German people is indicated by the way characters simultaneously notice and do not notice the smell that is coming from the bones.

5

TEETH AND SNAILS

After the appearance of *Dog Years* in 1963, there was a gap of six years before the publication of Grass's next novel *Local Anaesthetic*, but since much of the *Dog Years* material dates from the period 1956–60 when he was living in Paris, the gap was really more like ten years, and *Local Anaesthetic* is quite different, both in style and substance, from anything he had previously written. In the three fictions that derive their impetus from disillusionment with his parents' generation, Grass was siding with the boys against the grown-ups, but in 1968, when from its epicentre in Paris a quake of student rebellion spread over Europe, he was 38, and a new generation had grown up with no memory of Hitler or the war. If this generation had been betrayed, as it thought it had, it was by Grass and his contemporaries. Writing about the cruel laws of the Nazis and the order they had imposed so brutally, he had given free rein to the anarchic side of his own temperament; watching the students of 1968 give free rein to theirs, not in literature but on campus and in the streets, burning cars and books, Grass sympathized with the forces of law and order. 'It's basically an infantile attempt to prolong childhood,' he said of student radicalism in 1970, 'to hold on to the status of irresponsibility.'[18]

Not that this makes him unsympathetic in *Local Anaesthetic* towards Philipp Scherbaum, the student who is planning to soak his dachshund, Max, in petrol and burn him in the Kurfürstendamm to remind the fur-coated ladies who are munching cakes in Kempinski's that napalm is burning innocent Vietnamese people to an extremely painful death. Scherbaum is polite, highly intelligent, not at all fanatical; he believes that there is no need to accept the compromises of the older generation. Why should he settle for editing the student newspaper? Should he dedicate his energy to a campaign for having a smokers' corner behind the bicycle shed?

The teacher Eberhard Starusch, principal representative of the opposite viewpoint, is none other than Störtebeker, former leader of the 'Dusters', twenty years older. So in his arguments with his favourite pupil, he can point to his own rebellious past.

> What more can I say, Philipp? Even if you're right, it's not worth it. When I was seventeen, I myself. We were against everybody and everything. Same as you, I didn't want anything explained to me. I didn't want to turn into what I am now. Even if I am as I am and you see how I am, just as I saw how others were, I know that I've turned into something I don't want to be and that you don't want to be. But if I wanted to be the way you are, I'd have to say: Do it! Why don't I say: Burn him!? (*LA*, p. 183)

To put Scherbaum's plan into perspective, two other protest gestures are introduced into the story. Starusch remembers a former soldier, Schlottau, who joined a movement in the mid-1950s to protest against German rearmament. Going further back into history, Starusch tells the story of Bartholdy, a 17-year-old high school student who, during 1797, together with a few fellow students and Polish dock labourers, conspired in Danzig to overthrow the monarchy.

To some extent Grass is writing about the impossibility of living in the child-based counterworld he had realized in his first three fictions. The world of *Local Anaesthetic* is a more reasonable world, but, depending too heavily on dramatized reasoning, it does not spring full-bloodedly to life. This is a less visual, more verbal novel. There is only a word – 'pain' – to link toothache, which infallibly makes itself felt, with what Grass calls 'a stronger, abstract pain, like the war in Vietnam'.[19] This is all too easily forgotten by everyone except Scherbaum, and eventually even by him when he lets himself be distracted by the dental treatment he needs.

Dentistry stands for the principle of offering limited but real help by relieving pain, but the metaphor is overworked and Grass's biggest failure is with the dentist. Nothing in this argumentative novel is so vivid or so forceful as the best sequences in the early fiction, and after the painstaking but effective efforts to realize Oskar in a painterly way, Grass oddly chooses to leave the dentist, who is the chief carrier of the play's wisdom, not only nameless but also faceless. Implausibly, he finds time for innumerable conversations – on the telephone and in the surgery – to advise Starusch on what he should do about Scherbaum, and to expound his philosophy. When he argues that the principle of health insurance should be extended internationally, we are obviously intended to disagree, but we are expected to sympathize with his hostility to idealism, his insistence on the importance of making progress gradually.

While he is apparently immune to guilt about the Nazi past, Starusch's girlfriend, Irmgard Seifert, another teacher, is troubled by memories of her involvement in the League of German Girls. How could she possibly have thought it was right to put other people's lives at risk by denouncing them? How could she, at the age of 17, have arranged for 14-year-old boys to be trained in using such murderous weapons as the bazooka? Desperate to expiate her guilt, she naively encourages Scherbaum to go ahead with his dog-burning plan: his purity is exemplary; he will be her redeemer. As a character Irmgard is far less convincing than the younger girl who encourages Scherbaum. Vero Lewand is a left-wing reincarnation of Tulla Pokriefke, and in her militant fanaticism she does not stop short of seducing Starusch in order to discredit him.

Some of the book's symbols are cleverly contrived. Starusch is being treated by the dentist for a deformation of the jaw which makes him look determined while reducing the effectiveness of his bite. But the book might have had more bite if the determination behind it had been less apparent. It seems too schematic.

One of its most interesting features in Grass's postmodernist refusal to tell the story straightforwardly. This time we have only one narrator, but the narrative is fragmented into small units, as if Starusch were making hasty jottings in a diary. This creates a discontinuity which is sometimes valuable, but is irritating when the breathlessness seems mannered, as it often does, especially when Grass is smuggling flashbacks into the narrative under pretext of recording Starusch's wandering thoughts while he is staring at the television which the dentist has installed in his surgery (or 'office' as the American translation has it) to distract the patient from his pain. 'Even the empty screen can fade in the flow of your thoughts' (*LA*, p. 16). Thematically distraction from pain is relevant, but the Schlottau theme, which is developed in these flashbacks, does not emerge forcefully enough. Most of the first half of the book is concerned with Starusch's memories of a relationship with a former fiancée, Linde, and her father, Krings, owner of a cement factory and formerly a general, later field-marshal in Hitler's army. Schlottau is meant to serve as a point of comparison with Scherbaum, and Linde with Irmgard, but the first half of the book is pallid stuff, and the second half far more vivid, though not vivid enough.

*

The refusal to write straightforward narrative and the cult of discontinuity survive into the next book, *From the Diary of a Snail*, which followed in 1972; what is new is the idea of plaiting fictional and non-fictional strands together. In *Local Anaesthetic* there had been explicit references to the reigning German Chancellor, the ex-Nazi Kiesinger, when Starusch and Irmgard abrasively discussed him. But in *From the Diary of a Snail*, Grass is concerned not only with the current political situation in Germany but also with his own involvement in it.

In one sequence, questioned about commitment by students, he illustrates his daily life with two beermats.

'This is my political work that I do as a Social Democrat and citizen; this is my manuscript, my profession, my whatcha-callit.' I let the distance between the beer mats increase, moved them closer together, leaned one against the other, covered one with the other (then the other with the one) and said, 'Sometimes it's hard, but it can be done. You shouldn't worry so much.' (*DS*, p. 250)

But beermats do not interpenetrate and, despite an elaborate pattern of connections and correspondences, neither do the strands in the novel – if 'novel' is the right word for this book. The high proportion of non-fiction makes this questionable.

Though the storytelling impulse is strong, Grass's principal motivation, it seems, is to dramatize his own position as storyteller, political campaigner, father and famous man of letters. In *Local Anaesthetic* his characterization of Starusch was blurred by his uncertainty about how far to identify with him; subsequently Grass was disappointed that critics had failed to appreciate the irony that was meant to play against Starusch's willingness to accept the status quo. In *From the Diary of a Snail* the main character is unequivocally Günter Grass, and the main theme is the relationship between passivity and political action. Do melancholy and utopia preclude each other or fertilize each other? The central symbol, the snail, is used as dentistry is used in the previous novel – as emblematic of patience and slow, steady progress.

The book could almost be mistaken for a carefully edited transcript of notebooks kept by a rather self-conscious writer who, like Kafka, jots down fragments of fiction in his diary, mixed up with his account of everyday conversations and events. We see Grass in conversation with his four children who quiz him about himself and grumble about his protracted absences from home during the 1969 election campaign. We see him on trains and in cars, making speeches, signing auto-graphs and dealing with the people who accost him before and after meetings. We move in and out of the stories he is writing;

60

we even see him hesitating over choices to be made about characterization.

Though the quality of the writing is uneven, the general level is considerably higher than in *Local Anaesthetic*. The self-portraiture is enriched with a subtle blend of candour and self-irony. He tells us that his favourite flower is the light grey scepsis, which blooms all the year round, and that he needs supplies of tobacco, lentils and paper.

> In addition to telling stories and telling stories against stories, I insert pauses between half sentences, describe the gait of various kinds of snails, do not ride a bicycle or play the piano, but hew stone (including granite), mould damp clay, work myself into muddles (aid to developing countries, social policy), and cook pretty well (even if you don't like my lentils). I can draw left- or right-handed with charcoal, pen, chalk, pencil, and brush. That's why I'm capable of tenderness. I can listen, not listen, foresee what has happened, think until it unhappens, and – except when knotted string or scholastic speculations are being unravelled – have patience. But this much is certain: I used to be able to laugh a lot better. I pass some things over in silence: my gaps. Sometimes I'm sick of being alone and would like to crawl into something soft, warm, and damp, which it would be inadequate to characterize as feminine. How I wear myself out looking for shelter. (*DS*, pp. 66–7)

The main strand of fiction in the book is about a school-master, Hermann Ott, nicknamed Doubt. (Like the word 'pain' in the previous book, the word 'doubt' has a synthesizing function here.) Ott is not Jewish but teaches German and biology at a Jewish school in pre-war Danzig, and refuses to give up his post when persecution of the Jews intensifies. When, recalcitrantly, he goes on buying his vegetables from a Jewish greengrocer, the attitude of the ordinary citizen is nicely epitomized when 'a lovable little grandma pulled a hatpin out of her pot-shaped felt and thrust it once, and once again, into the green lettuce. "Shame!" she shouted, and wiped her hatpin on

61

her sleeve' (*DS*, p. 77). Eventually, after police interrogation and beatings, Ott escapes on his bicycle. On the road to Karthaus, noticing that his rear tyre is flat and unable to repair it, he makes for a cycle shop he has previously used. The shop-owner, Anton Stomma, hides him till the end of the war in his junk-filled cellar. Stomma often beats him, for no reason except that he enjoys it, but Ott also benefits from the quirky nature of Stomma, who sends his mute daughter, Elspeth, down to sleep with the man in the cellar. Ott entertains himself by collecting snails and entertains his hosts with dramatized readings from the classics. He makes the Prince of Homburg sleepwalk behind a sheet stretched between stored potatoes and dangling bicycle frames and, to play a variety of characters, Ott wears a variety of hats belonging to Stomma and his dead wife (*DS*, p. 177). The fiction gathers so much force that it is hard to believe Grass would have served it better by developing it into an independent novel or novella.

There are two other important strands in the book, one fictional and one non-fictional. The fiction – closely based on fact – is about August, a middle-aged pharmacist, who poisons himself at one of the election meetings. He had once been a member of the SS, later become a pacifist; he had been unable to laugh. His suicidal depressiveness links up with the non-fictional theme of melancholy. Invited to lecture at the celebrations for the 500th anniversary of Albrecht Dürer's birth, Grass decides to talk about his 1514 engraving *Melencolia I*. The lecture, titled 'On Stasis in Progress', is printed in full at the end of the book; earlier, contemplating the task ahead of him, Grass reflects on melancholy and makes jottings, which read almost like blank verse:

Saturn is her planet./She peddles sprouting potatoes and hair in the comb./On Sundays she commands us to remember the way to school and back./She collects buttons, defeats, letters, and (like Doubt) empty snail shells./She keeps a dog that has no appetite./When visitors come, she warms up gruel. (*DS*, p. 104)

When Ott leaves Danzig, he takes a reproduction of *Melencolia I* with him. Grass also contrives other links between the strands. He tells us that the untidiness of Raoul's room – Raoul is one of his children – gives him the idea for the untidiness in the cellar; the mute Elspeth is like a personification of melancholy; at one point Willy Brandt is equated with Doubt: 'Phases of hesitation, dispersion. He sees the important issues and relationships down to the smallest granule, but persons (even important ones) in a blur, through frosted glass. (When the frosted glass is removed and persons he had favoured turn against him, he is silent and hears his silence.)' (*DS*, p. 224).

Subtler and more important is the connection between Ott and Grass. Like the dentist in *Local Anaesthetic*, Ott is left visually vague and Grass even advises the reader not to form a picture of him, but this time there is good reason for the facelessness: we are free to project Grass's features on the blank space.

The tone for the correspondence between Grass and Ott is set by the continuous use of his nickname, Doubt. This reminds us of the imaginary flower, the pale grey scepsis and the hesitations which are recurrent in the autobiographical part of the narrative. These connect with the self-description and Grass's implicit identification of himself with the snail. This, together with its sexual symbolism, is both more apparent and more suggestive in the German text, for the word *Schnecke* means not only 'snail' but also 'slug'. Ott collects both, and one of the most beautiful developments in the story is the process by which Elspeth is cured of her muteness. Since her lover can never leave the cellar, she begins to bring him slugs she collects in the cemetery. Puzzled over an unidentifiable slug, he is frustrated by her inability to answer questions about where she found it but, as a gesture of tenderness, he has often put snails or slugs on her arm, and eventually, after a period of muttering and mumbling, she is able to speak again, though only when this slug is on her arm. Her father, convinced that the man in his cellar is a Jewish doctor, is not surprised to find his daughter cured (*DS*, pp. 213–14) but she eventually kills the slug which restored her speech.

In the lecture on Dürer's *Melencolia*, Grass discusses melancholy as a social phenomenon – which must have surprised his audience more than it surprises readers of his book, for here he brings his strands together, essayistically at least, if not novelistically. The engraving was 'testimony to a period of transition whose effects are still at work today' (*DS*, p. 260). Contemporary Marxists are utopians who insist that history can find its way through violence to social justice; the German statesman – Grass rightly leaves him unnamed – who 'shouldered the burden' of a nation's 'undiminished guilt' when he knelt at the site of the Warsaw ghetto, was more realistic: 'repentance as a social state of mind ... presupposes melancholy rooted in insight' (*DS*, p. 265). Alongside the liberation of the individual, the Renaissance had asserted his right to melancholy (*DS*, p. 264), a right denied by the modern utopians, with their insistence on collective strength through compulsory cheerfulness. This is the context in which we finally have to view both the suicide of the melancholy Augst, the ex-soldier who, like Schlottau, turned into a campaigner for peace, and the cure performed by a slug.

6

FLOUNDERING

Though *The Flounder* (1977) is a bigger book than *From the Diary of a Snail*, it is less important and less well written. Even if we discount the widely publicized announcement that Grass intended it as a present to himself for his fiftieth birthday, it is clear that the motivation behind it is insufficient. In all his previous novels he had been ingenious in finding ways of combining disparate material, using a variety of devices from the Metaphysical conceits of *The Tin Drum* to plaiting strands of fiction and non-fiction in *From the Diary of a Snail*. In *The Flounder* he is still interested in anomaly as a structural principle, but he uses it in a more slapdash way than ever before, like a careless cook, throwing in a little of every ingredient that happens to be at hand. What the novel lacks is a strong image comparable in centripetal force to Oskar Matzerath or the relationship between Amsel and Matern. Neither the talking fish nor the talkative narrator are sufficiently vivid or interesting.

The flounder vaguely represents the *Zeitgeist* which, according to Grass, is now turning towards women, after centuries of favouring male dominance. In the Grimms' fairy tale 'The Fisherman and His Wife', a prince, who has been transformed into a fish, goes on helping a poor fisherman by granting all his wishes until, prompted by his greedy wife, he asks for too much. In *Dog Years* there is a lake that contains a red-blazed calf which can talk on St John's Day (*DY*, p. 119); later we meet a soothsaying miller who presses a sack of flour against his ear to hear what the mealworms will prophesy (*DY*, p. 271). The talking flounder makes its first leap out of the sea when the immortal narrator is in his Neolithic incarnation. Advice from the fish helps to liberate him from the comfortable oppression of the three-breasted matriarchs, who use their own milk in their cooking and quell male recalcitrance by sticking a tit into the open mouth.

The narrative overflows with Rabelaisian jokes about cooking, food, digestion, farting and defecation. It has obviously occurred to Grass that many readers might have preferred fewer of these jokes, but he is eager to help the squeamish with a surfeit he expects to work therapeutically. Ilsebill, the narrator's wife, is admonished for being reluctant to study her excrement:

> 'That's because you were brought up unwisely and too well,' I said. For our fecal matter should be important to us and not repel us. It's not a foreign body. It has warmth. Nowadays it's being described again in books, shown in films, and painted in still lifes. It had been forgotten, that's all. Because as far as I can think back and look behind me, all the cooks (inside me) have inspected their feces and – in all my time-phases – mine as well. (*F*, pp. 235–4)

In many of the interviews he gave on the book's publication, Grass explained that he had wanted to illuminate areas which had been neglected by the historians, who had tended to ignore not only malnutrition but also cooking and eating habits. The introduction of the potato into Prussia – credited in the novel to one of the narrator's wives, Amanda Woyke – should have been recognized as a more important event than the Thirty Years War. In this rewriting of history, the Neolithic period was one of solitary eating and communal defecation. 'After the horde shit-together we felt collectively relieved and chatted happily, showing one another our finished products, drawing pithy comparisons with past performances, or teasing our

constipated comrades, who were still squatting in vain'
(*F*, p. 237). Convinced that there has been too much fas-
tidious reticence in four centuries of fiction, he tries, single-
handed, to redress the balance.

This is not the only way in which the book is over-ambitious.
Spanning the whole of human history, and reincarnating the
narrator in assorted guises, it tries to create a new myth about
the balance of power between the sexes. It was woman who
stole fire from the gods. Christianity was introduced as a means
of ending maternal absolutism; medieval scholasticism was
built up in order to exclude women. In the twentieth century
the male hegemony ends because the flounder finally tires of the
way men misuse the power he has given them.

> For centuries I did my best to hush up your defeats, to
> interpret your wretched failure as progress, to hide your now
> obvious ruin behind big buildings, drown it out with sym-
> phonies, beautify it in panel paintings on a golden back-
> ground, or talk it away in books, sometimes humorously,
> sometimes elegiacally, and sometimes, as a last resort, only
> intelligently. To prop up your superstructure I have even, in
> my desire to be helpful, invented gods, from Zeus to Marx.
> (*F*, pp. 149–50)

Twenty years ago it was unpredictable that Grass would ever
write prose as thin-blooded as this. A few poems are in-
terpolated into the narrative, but this time none of the prose is
poetic.

The sympathies of the fish now go to the feminists who, once
they have captured it, put it on trial, holding it responsible for
centuries of injustice. One strand in the fiction consists of the
flounder's statements to the tribunal, another of the stories the
narrator tells Ilsebill about her predecessors in his bed, another
of direct address to the reader. But whereas the strands in *From
the Diary of a Snail* were kept separate, these overlap. Grass
succeeds, more or less, in differentiating between the eleven
principal partners in the narrator's bed, but the attempt
to evoke contrasted historical backgrounds is an almost

unmitigated failure. The emphasis on food, digestion and elimination is partly jocular, but the balance between flippancy and seriousness has been disastrously upset. The structure is elaborate, and obviously Grass did a good deal of serious research but – protracted to 545 pages – the comedy could succeed only if it gave the feeling of life actually being lived.

Occasionally an episode does blaze into vividness. The narrator's fourth wife, Dorothea of Montau, who represents High Gothic religiosity, is preparing her penitential Lenten soup, kneeling ascetically on dried peas while codfish heads and mangels foam in the family-sized kettle. Concentrating devoutly on the crucifix, she does not notice that her 3-year-old daughter has fallen into the kettle. 'If the maid hadn't missed the child, she might have boiled away completely without disturbing her mother's fervour long enough for a Hail Mary' (F, pp. 125–6).

Though Grass is fluent in inventing incidents, few of them stand out as incisively as this one, and even here we are reminded of his roots in the *Neue Sachlichkeit*. As in a drawing by Georg Grosz, we are given caricature, not character, and the impression of rich detail is illusory.

7

CREATIVITY AND PROCREATION

Grass's next book, *The Meeting at Telgte*, shows that in *The Flounder* he had made little use of his talent for bringing a historical background richly to life, but this is another novella, written without either the formal precision or the deep commitment of *Cat and Mouse*. With his odd fixation on birthdays, Grass seems to have conceived *The Meeting at Telgte* as a present for the seventieth birthday of Hans Werner Richter, who had founded Gruppe 47 and taken the chair at its meetings. Set in 1647, 300 years before the group was founded and shortly before the Thirty Years War ended, the 130-page story invents a colloquium of writers in a Germany ravaged and depopulated by war, with little cohesive force left in a language which has itself been debased and impoverished. The parallel with the post-Hitler situation is clear enough, and the story raises the question of how much writers can do for their language and for their country.

Johann Jakob Christoffel von Grimmelshausen, the man who had most effectively translated the Thirty Years War into fiction, writing a series of novels which prefigured the *Bildungsroman* and profoundly influenced Grass, appears in the story not as a writer but as a soldier commanding a detachment of imperial horsemen and musketeers. By finding alternative lodgings for the writers when their original plan is upset, and by procuring enough meat for a banquet, when food is scarce, he contributes more to the conference than any of the writers who read from their work, criticize the work of others and discuss the state of the language. Not without thinking of himself, Grass is weighing action against literature, and championing an anti-literary writer who wrote well. In his parting tirade he promises the established writers that they will hear from him again:

> True, years and years might pass before he had refurbished his knowledge, bathed in Harsdörffer's sources, studied Moscherosch's craft, gleaned rules from this and that treatise, but then he would be present: as lively as you please, though tucked away in countless printed pages. But let no one expect mincing pastorals, conventional obituaries, complicated figure poems, sensitive soul-blubber, or well-behaved rhymes for church congregations. No, he would let every foul smell out of the bag; a chronicler, he would bring back the long war as a word-butchery, let loose gruesome laughter, and give the language license to be what it is: crude and soft-spoken, whole and stricken, here Frenchified, there melancolicky, but always drawn from the casks of life. (*MT*, pp. 117–18)

In fact Grimmelshausen, who was 25 in 1647, wrote his novels in the last ten years of his life (1666–76). *Das abenteuerliche Simplicissimus Teutsch* appeared in 1669, followed, the same year, by *Trutz Simplex: Oder Ausführliche und wunderseltzame Lebensbeschreibung der Erzbetrügerin und Landstörtzerin Courasche*. The central character, who had made her first appearance in the fifth book of *Simplicissimus*, reappears as Mutter Courage in Brecht's play, which covers the years 1624–36, and again in Grass's novella, where she is the landlady of the inn picked by Grimmelshausen (or Gelnhausen as he is called throughout most of the story) as the venue for the conference. He has been her lover, but she mocks at his intention of writing.

> Did he, Stoffel, the simple-minded regimental secretary, think he could compete with the art of the learned gentlemen

now gathered in her house? . . . Did he, whose mouth over-flowed with foolishness, hope to keep pace with Master Gryphius's verbal cascade, with the eloquent wisdom of Johann Rist? No, really, did he think he could rival the daring, lavishly ornamented wit of Masters Harsdörffer and Moscherosch? Had he, whom no magister had taught how to put a sentence together or count feet, the gall to measure his metric skill with that of the acute Master Logau? Did he, who didn't even know what religion he believed in, suppose he could drown out Master Gerhardt's pious hymns? Did he, who had started life as a wagoner and stableboy, then turned common soldier, and only lately risen to the rank of regimental secretary, he who had never learned anything but murder, robbing corpses, highway robbery, and perhaps in a pinch the art of keeping regimental records, aspire to make his way with hymns and sonnets with witty and entertaining satires, odes, and elegies? (*MT*, p. 106)

The other familiar name that presents itself in the novella is Heinrich Schütz. An uninvited but honoured guest, the composer listens greedily to the verse that is read out. His music is designed to serve and enhance the written word, but until now he has limited himself mainly to the Latin liturgy and to Luther's Bible. Sadly he concludes that most of these poets are too prolix.

The first half of the novella, like the first half of *Local Anaesthetic*, is inferior to the second, but as a whole, *The Meeting at Telgte* is more satisfactory than anything Grass had written since *Dog Years*, though it cannot be said to fulfil the promise of the early work.

*

Like *From the Diary of a Snail*, Grass's most recent book, *Headbirths, or the Germans Are Dying Out* (1980) mixes diary material with fiction, but the writing is less incisive and the construction sloppier.

Max Frisch, who is more skilful than Grass at carving works

of art out of diary material, distinguishes between the 'I' in fiction, which is a figure, and the 'I' in a diary, which is an attribution. 'To have a figure you must also know what it is concealing, what doesn't interest it at the moment, what it is not aware of, etc. . . . Unabashed first person writers like Henry Miller, Witold Gombrowicz etc. are not writing confessions, and are bearable because the "I" of their works assumes the quality of a role.'[20] It is only in Grass's first three fictions that the 'I' is wholeheartedly figured. In *The Meeting at Telgte* he halfheartedly tries to spin a mystery around the narrator's identity. In *Headbirths, or the Germans Are Dying Out*, as in *From the Diary of a Snail*, the 'I' is an attribution, and in *The Flounder* he takes an obvious and rather suspect pleasure in identifying with the virile male who relishes every corner of physicality and beds virtually every woman in the book.

Self-consciousness has been problematic in all Grass's fiction since *Dog Years*. Even in *The Meeting at Telgte*, where it is least damaging, it is apparent in his championship of an unlettered man of action against the literati. It is most damaging in *Headbirths*, where it leads to such flabby prose as

> This much is clear: we won't shoot the picture in China, even if Schlöni, as our children call him, gets permission. In the People's Republic, they've eliminated starvation, made dying a little less compulsive, and by an enormous effort (though too late) brought the urge to be born under control. Only the first child is subsidized. When a second child is born, the subsidy for the first child is withdrawn. If Chinese parents dare to bring a third child into the world, they have to repay all sums received for the first. (*H*, p. 58)

It would be possible, obviously, to write a good story about China, highlighting the emotional and psychological repercussions of the state's financial intervention in family planning. Instead, Grass is content to comment sardonically from the sidelines. Should the West present China with 500,000 psychiatrists to combat the neuroses and complexes that must be induced? What would Germany be like if the population rose to parity with the Chinese – 950 million? But the story he was intending to write for Volker Schlöndorff was about a German couple, Harm and Dörte Peters – the latest in Grass's long line of schoolteachers – who are trying, while travelling through over-populated countries in Asia, to reach agreement about whether to have a baby. While collecting the material which he serves up, undercooked, in *Headbirths*, Grass was himself travelling through Asia with his new wife, Ute, and the Schlöndorffs. As in *From the Diary of a Snail*, he shows himself hesitating over alternatives in the fiction he is assembling, and shows how personal experiences produce usable notions. But while the snail-collecting Ott becomes a vivid, three-dimensional figure, Grass makes little effort to characterize the teachers or to paint pictures: 'If I neglect the features of Harm and Dörte Peters, outfitting him with no squint and her with no gap between her front teeth, it's for a reason. Schlöndorff will fill in these clearly circumscribed blanks with the facial expressions of two actors' (*H*, p. 99). But Schlöndorff decided against making the film, which would have had to depend too heavily on a series of reaction shots to show the teachers' feelings about the squalour and suffering they observe. They did not become sufficiently involved and, according to Schlöndorff, a cinema audience would have been less interested in what they saw in the streets than in what they did in their hotel bedroom.[21]

Instead of going back to his fiction and using language to fill in the blanks, Grass, relying on his reputation and on the reader's tolerance, presents a less carefully planned mixture of fact and fiction than he had ever previously marketed. Reflections on the political situation in Germany jostle against observations of India and Bali. Self-indulgently, he fantasizes about what he would do if he were given dictatorial powers. Sentimentally he takes us into his confidence about a dying friend, the writer Nicolas Born. Interestingly, he describes an attempt to preserve the spirit of Gruppe 47 by arranging meetings at which writers from East and West Berlin read from work in progress (*H*, p. 63).

But the author of *Headbirths* could hardly be more different from the young writer who spent a year studying the history of the *novella* before he penned *Cat and Mouse*. During his self-imposed Parisian exile (1956–60) there was nothing to distract Grass from pouring all his formidable energy into literature, but since his return to West Germany, allowing himself to be sidetracked repeatedly into political campaigning, he has failed to fulfil the promise that was implicit in his first three fictions.

Superficially this might seem surprising. Shouldn't he have been able to cull valuable material from practical experience in everyday politics? Shouldn't he have gained useful insights into how countries are run and how elections are won? Wasn't his commitment to the Social Democrats a logical extension of his retrospective hostility to the Nazis?

Discussing Emile Zola's *Truth*, the novel which ought to have benefited from his courageous involvement in the Dreyfus affair, Henry James remarked: 'Nothing was ever so odd as that these great moments should appear to have been wasted, when all was said, for his creative intelligence. *Vérité* . . . is a production unrenewed and unrefreshed by them, spreads before us as somehow flatter and greyer, not richer and more relieved by reason of them.'[22] To explain why Zola's imagination was not stimulated by political experience, James suggests that he was too old; Grass was not, but his imagination was no longer racing as it had when he needed literature as an outlet for his rage against the grown-ups. All his best inventions are centred on a child-based counterworld; as soon as he cantered into the political tilting-yard, with the emblems of the snail and the dentist blazoned on his pennant, his writing became less forceful. None of his later work is sufficiently incisive to exert influence on the younger generation of writers.

But the first three fictions are still influential, and it is on these that his achievement depends. Together with Gabriel Garcia Marquez, Grass is an avatar of magical realism, a strain which finds its way into a variety of fiction by younger writers all over the world. One example is Botho Strauss's 1984 novel *The Young Man*, which has some of its roots in Novalis, German Romanticism and the fairy-tales which became a vehicle for allegory. But *The Tin Drum* had pointed the way – backwards and forwards.

NOTES

1 Volker Schlöndorff, in an interview with Ronald Hayman, 8 November 1984.
2 'Not Only a Writer', interview with Günter Grass on *24 Hours*, BBC television, 23 September 1969.
3 Heinrich von Kleist, letter to August Rühle von Lilienstern, 3 August 1906.
4 Heinrich von Kleist, *Sämtliche Werke* (Droemer, 1954), p. 888.
5 Rolf Geissler (ed.), *Günter Grass: Materialienbuch* (Neuwied: Luchterhand, 1976), p. 26.
6 *Aufsätze zur Literatur* (Neuwied: Luchterhand, 1980), p. 7.
7 Samuel Johnson, *Prefaces, Biographical and Critical, to the Works of the English Poets: Abraham Cowley* (London, 1779–81).
8 Interview with Ronald Hayman, *Encounter* (September 1970); repr. in *Playback 2* (London: Davis Poynter, 1973).
9 John Reddick, *The Danzig Trilogy of Günter Grass* (London: Secker & Warburg, 1975).
10 Ibid., pp. 99–100.
11 Schlöndorff interview.
12 'Not Only a Writer'.
13 Reddick, op. cit., *passim*.
14 Walter Höllerer, quoted in ibid.
15 Interview with John Reddick, ibid., p. 158.
16 'Not Only a Writer'.
17 Reddick, op. cit., pp. 267–70.
18 Interview in *Playback 2*.
19 Ibid.
20 Max Frisch, *Sketchbook 1966–71*, trans. Geoffrey Skelton (London: Methuen, 1974).
21 Schlöndorff interview.
22 Henry James, *The Art of Fiction and Other Essays* (New York: Oxford University Press, 1948), p. 177.

BIBLIOGRAPHY

WORKS BY GÜNTER GRASS

Novels

Die Blechtrommel. Neuwied: Luchterhand, 1959. Trans. Ralph Manheim as *The Tin Drum.* London: Secker & Warburg, 1961. New York: Random House, 1964.

Katz und Maus. Neuwied: Luchterhand, 1961. Trans. Ralph Manheim as *Cat and Mouse.* London: Secker & Warburg, 1963. New York: Harcourt Brace, 1963.

Hundejahre. Neuwied: Luchterhand, 1963. Trans. Ralph Manheim as *Dog Years.* London: Secker & Warburg, 1965. New York: Harcourt Brace, 1963.

Örtlich betäubt. Neuwied: Luchterhand, 1969. Trans. Ralph Manheim as *Local Anaesthetic.* London: Secker & Warburg, 1970. New York: Harcourt Brace, 1969.

Aus dem Tagebuch einer Schnecke. Neuwied: Luchterhand, 1972. Trans. Ralph Manheim as *From the Diary of a Snail.* London: Secker & Warburg, 1974. New York: Harcourt Brace, 1973.

Der Butt. Neuwied: Luchterhand, 1977. Trans. Ralph Manheim as *The Flounder.* London: Secker & Warburg, 1978. New York: Harcourt Brace, 1978.

Das Treffen in Telgte. Neuwied: Luchterhand, 1979. Trans. Ralph Manheim as *The Meeting at Telgte.* London: Secker & Warburg, 1981. New York: Harcourt Brace, 1981.

Kopfgeburten oder Die Deutschen sterben aus. Neuwied: Luchterhand. Trans. Ralph Manheim as *Headbirths, or The Germans Are Dying Out.* London: Secker & Warburg, 1982. New York: Harcourt Brace, 1982.

Verse

Die Vorzüge der Windhühne. Neuwied: Luchterhand, 1956.
Gleisdreieck. Neuwied: Luchterhand, 1970.

Selected Poems. German text with trans. by Michael Hamburger and Christopher Middleton. London: Secker & Warburg, 1966. New York: Harcourt Brace, 1966.

Ausgefragt. Neuwied: Luchterhand, 1967.

New Poems. German text with trans. by Michael Hamburger. New York: Harcourt Brace, 1968.

Gesammelte Gedichte. Neuwied: Luchterhand, 1971.

In the Egg and Other Poems. German text with trans. by Michael Hamburger and Christopher Middleton. London: Secker & Warburg, 1978.

'Ach Butt, dein Märchen geht böse aus': Gedichte und Radierungen. Neuwied: Luchterhand, 1983.

Plays

Hochwasser. Frankfurt: Suhrkamp, 1963.

Onkel, Onkel. Berlin: Wagenbach, 1965.

Die Plebejer proben den Aufstand. Neuwied: Luchterhand, 1966. Trans. Ralph Manheim as *The Plebeians Rehearse the Uprising.* London: Secker & Warburg, 1967. New York: Harcourt Brace, 1966.

Four Plays: Flood, Mister Mister, Only Ten Minutes to Buffalo and *The Wicked Cooks.* Trans. Ralph Manheim and A. Leslie Willson. London: Secker & Warburg, 1968. New York: Harcourt Brace, 1967.

Davor. Theater heute, 10, 4 (1969).

Theaterspiele: Hochwasser, Onkel, Onkel, Noch zehn Minuten bis Buffalo, Die bösen Köche, Die Plebejer proben den Aufstand, Davor. Neuwied: Luchterhand, 1970.

Beritten hin und zurück: Ein Vorspiel auf dem Theater. Akzente, 5 (1958). Trans. Michael Benedikt and Joseph Goradza as *Rocking Back and Forth* in Michael Benedikt and Georg Wellworth (eds), *Postwar German Theatre.* New York: Dutton, 1967.

Critical, political and miscellaneous

Die Ballerina. Berlin: Friedenauer Presse, 1963.

Über das Selbstverständliche. Neuwied: Luchterhand, 1968.

Über meiner Lehrer Döblin und andere Vorträge. Berlin: Literarisches Colloquium, 1968.

Dokumente zur politischen Wirkung (ed. Heinz Ludwig Arnold and Franz Jose Görtz). Munich: Richard Boorberg Verlag, 1971.

Der Bürger und seine Stimme. Reden-Aufsätze-Kommentare. Neuwied: Luchterhand, 1974.

Denkzettel: Politische Reden und Aufsätze 1965–76. Neuwied:
Luchterhand 1978.
Speak Out! Speeches, Open Letters, Commentaries. Trans. Ralph
Manheim. London: Secker & Warburg, 1969. New York: Harcourt Brace, 1969.
Aufsätze zur Literatur. Neuwied: Luchterhand, 1980.
Widerstand Lernen: Politische Gegenreden 1980–1983. Neuwied:
Luchterhand, 1984.

Graphic work

Dreher, Anselm (ed.). *Zeichnungen und Texte 1954–77 (Zeichnen
und Schreiben Bd I).* Neuwied: Luchterhand, 1982.

BIBLIOGRAPHY

Everett, George A. *A Selected Bibliography of Günter Grass* (1956–
73). New York: Burt Franklin, 1974.
Görtz, Franz Josef. 'Kommentierte Auswahl-Bibliographie'. In Heinz
Ludwig Arnold (ed.), 'Günter Grass'. *Text u. Kritik*, 1/1 (1978).
O'Neill, Patrick. *Günter Grass: A Bibliography 1955–75.* Toronto:
University of Toronto Press, 1976.

SELECTED CRITICISM OF GÜNTER GRASS

Arnold, Heinz Ludwig (ed.). 'Günter Grass'. *Text u. Kritik*, 1/1
(1978).
Cunliffe, W. G. *Günter Grass.* New York: Twayne, 1969.
Frisch, Max. *Sketchbook 1966–71.* Trans. Geoffrey Skelton,
pp. 253–60. London: Methuen, 1974.
Geissler, Rolf (ed.). *Günter Grass: Materialienbuch.* Neuwied:
Luchterhand, 1976.
Görtz, Franz Josef (ed.). *Günter Grass: Auskunft für Leser.* Neuwied:
Luchterhand, 1984.
Hollington, Michael. *Günter Grass: The Writer in a Pluralist Society.*
London: Marion Boyars, 1980.
Leonard, Irène. *Günter Grass.* Edinburgh: Oliver & Boyd, 1974.
Loschütz, Gerd (ed.). *Von Buch zu Buch: Günter Grass in der Kritik.*
Neuwied: Luchterhand, 1968.
Miles, Keith. *Günter Grass.* London: Vision, 1975.
O'Neill, Patrick. 'The Scheherezade Syndrome: Günter Grass's
Meganovel *Der Butt*'. In Getrud Bauer Pickar (ed.), *Adventures
of a Flounder: Critical Essays on Günter Grass's 'Der Butt'.*
Munich: Fink, 1982.

Reddick, John. *The Danzig Trilogy of Günter Grass*. London: Secker & Warburg, 1975.

Subiotto, Arrigo. 'Günter Grass'. In *Essays on Contemporary German Men of Letters*. London: Wolff, 1966.

Tank, Kurt Lothar. *Günter Grass*. New York: Ungar, 1969.

Thomas, R. Hinton and Van der Will, W. *The German Novel and the Affluent Society*. Manchester: Manchester University Press, 1968.

Willson, A. Leslie (ed.). *A Günter Grass Symposium*. Austin, Tex.: University of Texas Press, 1971.